THROUGH DARKNESS:
A Story of the Bosnian Diaspora

Aldiana Deumic

DEDICATION

For my two daughters Almedina and Aminela, my best friend, my husband Amir Deumić, my parents, my sister as well as my relatives, friends, neighbors and all other victims of cruelty and war who are struggling to find inner peace and those whose lives were taken too soon.

TABLE OF CONTENTS:

ACKNOWLEDGMENTS

First of all I would like to thank God for answering my prayers and for giving me a second chance at life. I am blessed to be alive and to have a healthy and a beautiful family in spite of all that I had lived. Dear God thank you for watching over me and for listening to my prayers.

To my mom and to my dad, who raised me to live with strong beliefs in humanity, compassion, patience, tolerance, hard work, honesty and ethics- thank you for instilling in me the belief that the education is the key to success.

To my love, my confidant, my best friend, Amir Deumic, thank you for being there for me and believing in me. Thank you for being my moral support and my positive energy.

Almedina and Aminela, my darlings, my sunshine and my life — it is two of you that I must thank the most. You believed in me more than I believed in myself. You are my light, and my happiness, my inner peace, and mommy and daddy will love you always unconditionally.

I want to thank my sister Arijana Gredelj for supporting me on this book since the day one. I also want to thank her for her vivaciousness and her humor.

Muhammed Al-Ahari, a man who dedicates his life to teaching at a challenging school, studying writing and publishing work — thank you for editing the novel.

To a young man with extreme artistic talent, excellent listening skills, Fahrudin Omerović, a huge thank you for your creativity and help on designing the cover of this novel.

Kate Hogan, a very intelligent and noble girl,

an enormous thank you for reading an earlier draft of novel and giving me excellent suggestions and recommendations on how to make it better. Thank you for helping my dreams come true!

An immense thank you, to my Aunt Besima and Uncle Asim Horić for taking us into their home as refugees, for feeding us, clothing us, and providing for us during the harshest times. I will never forget what you   did   for   us.

Most importantly thanks to those who gave their lives to defend us, so that we could have a second chance at life--same those who died unnaturally: Ibrahim Sabanović, Hamza Culic, Brajko Music, Nurija Pehlivanović and Fatima Music. May God give you peace to your souls! You will never be forgotten!

And finally, a huge thank you to the rest of my family members; my grandmother, my aunts, my cousins, my friends, my neighbors, and all of those who had helped me and believed in me.

CHARACTER GUIDE

AMNA- Ahm-nah (the narrator)
SARA- narrator's younger daughter
HANA- narrator's first daughter
JAAN- (narrator's husband)
LAMIJA- Lah-mee-yah (narrator's younger sister)
SABIRA- Sah-bee-rah (narrator's mom)
ADEM- Ah-deh-m (narrator's father)
RAZIJA- Rah-zee-yah (narrator's mother-in-law)
SALIM- Sah-lee-m (narrator's father-in law)
ADELA- narrator's cousin
JUSUF- Yuh-suh-f (narrator's cousin)
AUNT AMIRA- Ah-mee-rah (Grandmother Zineta's sister)
NANA FATIMA- Nah-nah Fah-tee-mah (narrator's fraternal grandma)
GRANDFATHER ADIL- Ah-dee-l (fraternal grandpa)
NANA ZINETA- Zee-neh-tah (narrator's maternal grandma)
GRANDFATHER ASIM- Ah-see-m (maternal granpa)
AMEL- Ah-meh-l (narrator's first cousin)
AMIDJA ONUR- Ah-mee-jah Oh-nuh-r (narrator's father's brother)
JOHN-neighbor
SONYA & MARKO-NEIGHBORS- Serbian neighbors in Chicago
JOSIP BROZ TITO- Yoh-see-p Brohz Teetoh (the ex-ruler of Yugoslavia)
JASMINA- Yas-mee-nah (a girl with make-up)
ADIS- Ah-dee-s (little boy/Ivan's kumche)
IVAN & IVANA- Croat soldier and his daughter
LALA & AMAR- Lah-lah and Ah-mah-r (recently married couple)

8

SOFIA- Croatian neighbor
LARISA- Lah-ree-ssah (girl from concentration camp)
SALIMA- Sah-lee-mah (women from concentration camp)
DANA-Dja-nah (small girl in the camp)
TETKA NAJLA- Nah-y-lah (narrator' mom's sister)
AJLA- Ah-y-la-h (Najla's daughter)
UNCLE HADIS- Hah-dee-s (Ajla's husband)
AUNT SHEILA- Onur's wife, Amel's and Amir's mom
TETKA AMINA- Ah-mee-neh (father's oldest sister)
UNCLE ENES- Ah-neh-s (Amina's husband)
SAMIA- first cousin, Amina's and Enes' daughter
AUNT IRMA- Uncle Nair's wife
UNCLE NAIL- Nah-ee-l (mother's brother)
HAMZA- Hah-m-zah (man from the river)
TETKA BERINA- Beh-ree-nah (father's sister)
UNCLE AHMED- Ah-h-meh-d (Berina's husband)
ADNA- Ah-d-nah (Berina's and Ahmed's daughter
ADNAN-Ah-d-nah-n (Berina's and Ahmed's son)
AMILA-Ah-mee-lah (Adnan's wife)
TETKA ASYA- Ah-s-yah (father's sister)
UNCLE MUHAMED (Asya's husband)
KAMIL- Kah-mee-l (Asya's and Muhamed's oldest son)
ADAN- Ah-dah-n (Asya's and Muhamed's middle child)
HARUN- Hah-roo-n (Asya's and Muhamed's youngest son)
UNCLE SMAIL-S-mah-ee-l (mom's brother)
AUNT SENADA-She-nah-dah (Smail's wife)
ENIS- Eh-nee-s (soldier)
MIKI- Mee-kee (Samia's boyfriend)
FARUK- Fah-ruh-k (boy from hospital)
AUNT LEILA- father's youngest sister

UNCLE BESIM- Leila's husband
YASIN- Leila's and Besim's son
MARIA- Croatian lady in Zenica
ZEHRA- Zeh-h-rah (girl from Kozarac)
AZRA, AMRA AND AJNA- friends from Vranduk
AUNT AISHA- Ah-ee-shah (Grandma Zineta's sister)
UNCLE SAID- Sah-ee-d (Aisa's husband)
FRANK- Croat soldier
HAFIZA- Hah-fee-zah (woman from Srebrenica)
ZLATA- young girl from Srebrenica
ALIYA- girl from Zepa
MAIDA- girl from Zepa
ADA- Uncle Ahmed's old grandma
MILAN & DRAGAN- Serbian brothers
ANITA- Mexican friend
BELMA- Jaan's cousin
MERISA- friend from school
MAHIR- Lamija's husband
EMRAH- Lamija's and Mahir's
AMELA- Adan' wife
JASMIN- Adna's husband
EMINA- Adna's and Jasmin's daughter
ILMA- Adan's and Amela's daughter
HARIS- Ajla's husband
ALI- Ajla's and Haris's son
EDIN- Aisha's son
DINA- Amir's wife
AYDIN- Ah-y-dee-n (Berina's and Ahmed's youngest son)
SADIA- Sah-dee-ah (Kamil's wife)
EDINA- Eh-dee-nah (Kamil's daughter

GEOGRAPHIC LOCATION GUIDE

Zepce- Zh-eh-bh-che
Berek- Beh-reh-kh
Preko- Ph-reh-koh
Previla- Phreh-vee-lah
Hrastusa- Hrah-stuh-shah
Orlovik- Ohr-love-week
Zeleca- Zh-eh-leh-cha
Golubinja- Goh-luh-bee-nyah
Begov Han- Beh-gohvh Hah-nh
Topcic Polje- Toh-bh-cheech Poh-lyeh
Nemila- Neh-mee-lah
Vranduk- Vrah-nh-duh-kh
Zenica- Zeh-nee-tzah
Perkovici- Peh-rh-koh-vee-chee
Kozarac- Koh-zah-rah-tz
Manjaca- Mah-nya-chah
Omarska- Oh-mahr-skah
Keraterm- Keh-rah-the-rhm
Srebrenica- Sreh-breh-nee-tza
Zepa- Zh-eh-bh-ah
Prjedor- Ph-rh-yeh-door
Trnopolje- Th-rh-noh-poh-lyeh
Seher- She-hehr

PROLOGUE

Nee-nah-nee-nah....takka-takka-takka- takka-takka...rat-a-tat-rat-a-tat bvoom...wham-sssshblam!!!!!!!...

Why did the war in the former Yugoslavia start? What led to it? Who was responsible for it? Who benefitted by it? How many innocent lives were taken? How many young girls were forcefully raped, beaten and killed? How many of them were impregnated? How many of these harmless maidens were nine, ten, eleven, twelve, thirteen, fourteen, fifteen, sixteen and seventeen? How many were mass raped by were-men they used to look up to before? How many mothers watched their daughters get beaten and raped? How many moms and daughters were raped simultaneously by same soldiers at the same time? How many grandmothers were made fun of and forced to perform sexual acts on drunken men? How many innocent Muslim and non-Muslim people were shot and died during the war? How many throats were cut with knives? How many boys, girls, infants, mothers, fathers, grandfathers, grandmothers, aunts, uncles, neighbors were burned alive? How many of them stepped on land mines and died as a result? How many of them starved to death? How many innocent lives were taken while standing in lines to get water and food? How many people were shot while trying to swim and escape from concentration camps? How many young boys were left handicapped? How many of them lost their legs, their arms, their hands, their fingers, their eyes? How many homes were burned, shelled? How much money the enemy made by selling their neighbors furniture, gold, and other valuables? Who profited and who lost? How many innocent lives and those

12

defending their loved ones are still buried in mass graves? How many of them are still missing? Who is still suffering and how? How many people committed suicides, during and after war and why? How many of them became addicted to alcohol, and drugs? How many war survivors received therapy and help? How many of them healed? How many victims are trying to heal and find peace and how? Who is helping survivors and how? If not, what will happen to survivors?

How many mass graves are found daily? How did the world react to the genocide that happened in Srebrenica, and other cities in Bosnia and Herzegovina? Do people still remember this? Do they care about it? Are we going to learn something from evil wars and Bosnia in particular? Are we going to do anything to help those who are in need?— those that are innocent? Are we going to take action and try to create a better world for our children, grandchildren and their children? I don't know why the war in Ex-Yugoslavia started. I was only nine. This is what I heard from other grownups:

The war in Bosnia and Herzegovina started on the April 5th, 1992, when the Serbs fired snipers on 100,000 individual rallying for peace in Sarajevo. Things got messy in February of 1992. Bosnia and Herzegovina announced that it wanted to become independent and break away from the Serb-dominated Yugoslavia. Bosnians and Croats backed this independence — but the Serbs were against it. That is when the Serbs decided to take things into their hands and snipers fired on the people gathering and backing peace.

Later on, Croats realized that they could take advantage of the war too — so they turned against their neighbors and friends as well. Sarajevo was targeted with over 1,000,000 missiles killing 11541 citizens, among them 1600 innocent children.

This began the longest military siege in a modern history of mankind. The Serbian siege of Sarajevo lasted 44 months. In 1995, in Srebrenica, located in Eastern Bosnia, 8000 men including boys as young as twelve were mass murdered in the biggest genocide since the World War II in Europe.

Others say that it all started after President Tito's death, and the fall of the Socialist/Communist dynasty. They say that his death led to the social and political crisis. When Tito was alive everyone on Balkans, located in Eastern Europe lived in peace, brotherhood, unity and love for one another. Yugoslavia, as it was called was located by the Adriatic Sea, just across the Italy.

Before 1990s, religion wasn't a problem. You were free to practice any religion you liked, or not practice at all — but you also respected other faiths. Yes, there are also those who say that Tito's Dynasty was bad. I don't know. All I heard was that during Josip Broz Tito's Dynasty, Croatia, Slovenia, Bosnia and Herzegovina, Serbia, Macedonia and Montenegro were all united. After his death, things started falling apart.

The year I was born, 1984, Sarajevo hosted Olympics. People say that President Tito was respected and liked by all world leaders during that time. I was young, and I don't recall any of it. All I remember is that before the war, I had a normal, happy childhood. I don't know the number of those that were raped, killed, wounded, and starved to death. I don't know what the future will bring. All I know, and all I can share are my childhood memories and stories of others victimized, murdered and hurt by the war. This is a story of inhumanity — cruelty —

loss — death — trauma — love — hope — and perseverance.

It is estimated that 100,000-110,000 Bosnian men, women and children were killed in the period from April 6th, 1992 to September 14th, 1995. More than two million women, children and men were displaced as refugees.

CHAPTER 1:
Bosnia 2001

It was June—the month of darkness—the longest, the most petrifying and the most difficult month for me— when all the scars hurt the most and the thunders of the unstoppable rain last the entire thirty days; side by side, with the throbbing skeletal and absorbing memory and information system pressure, and pains. My family and I went to visit our relatives back in Bosnia. Our hearts ached with extreme nostalgia. Even though our lives had improved significantly, we missed our loved ones. Our dream was to stay in the United States of America for a couple years to save some money, and to return to our motherland to try to rebuild our lives after the war.

My dad had worked hard. We managed to save ten thousand dollars, which was what we needed for plane tickets, some minor gifts to our family members, and money to spend for a month back home. The airfare tickets were more than a thousand dollars per person. I have managed to save a thousand dollars on my own.

During my freshman year, I started working part time after school and on the weekends. I tutored during summer time and worked the register at a local grocery store. I was young, smart and I didn't want to wait for my parents to give me allowance. It was the least I could do for my family. My mom and my dad had been sending money to Bosnia every month. They were supporting both of my grandma's since they had limited income. Both Grandma Fatima and Grandma Zineta received a small amount from grandfathers' pensions. This money wasn't enough for groceries. Most medications were very pricey, and weren't covered by insurance.

Seniors, disabled and sick war survivors, as well as the mothers and children of the killed men received limited assistance. Those Bosnian war survivors that stayed in Bosnia lived poorly. Many of them lost their homes and apartments during the war, and were living as refugees all over. The war had led to extreme economic problems. There were no jobs, no opportunities. A lot of people left the country and went to live and work in Diaspora—Germany, Austria, England, France, Slovenia, Denmark, Norway, the Netherlands, America and Australia.

War survivors and refugees that were left in Bosnia lived from the mercy of their neighbors, friends and family members, both who lived in Bosnia, but also those that were lucky to get out. The government did very little to help innocent, hurt, startled and disillusioned people who lost everything. The greedy became greedier, the corrupt became more corrupt, and the poor poorer. As a result most young people turned to drugs, alcohol, gambling, gangs, and trouble.

The thousand dollars that I worked hard to earn and save lasted me only three weeks. After we came to the United States, I wrote letters to my childhood best friends on a bi-monthly basis, and I called them at least monthly. The long distance calls at that time were pricey. We didn't have Facebook, Twitter, MySpace, MSN Messenger or Skype. I wanted to keep our friendship alive regardless of the distance. I was willing to go all the way. I knew finding true friends wasn't easy. I believed that my true friends were there, in Bosnia.

My friends, on the other hand, had seemed to be fine without me. They liked reading my lengthy letters, but they had difficulty responding. Perhaps, it was the postage fee, or the fact that they found other friends easily. Whatever the case, I went to Bosnia, ready to give them another chance, ready to spend my time and money with them. A week before we left Bosnia, my three friends from Vranduk came to visit me in Zepce. I had spent all my money already, so I asked my Grandma Fatima to lend me five German marks, so that my friends could pay their bus fare.

Nonetheless, this was the coolest summer of my life. My dad was pretty cool and easygoing. I didn't have a curfew. I went to cafés, some dance clubs, and was allowed to spend the nights in Vranduk at my friends' houses. One time we even went to Zenica and another city on our own.

The first week in Bosnia, after almost three years, wasn't what I had expected. I had been disappointed, saddened and shocked by the way people acted, talked and lived.

Back in Chicago, I hadn't seen any drugs at all, even though we lived in a ghetto neighborhood. I had attended a ghetto school, but I didn't come into contact with drugs. Here, in my own backyard, I was asked by my closest cousin, my brother from an uncle, Amel, to try weed. *"Amna do you want me to show you something cool? Come on upstairs! There is something in the attic that I want to show you,"* Amel added excitedly. He was sure that this was something that I might be interested in. After all, I was living in America. This must be normality for me.

"Ok, Amel let me see what you got up there," I said curiously. As I walked up the stairs, and entered the dark attic, I saw some green plants. *"What is that? Isn't this some kind of herb that you are growing? What does it do?" I bet this is your new invention! I bet this tea cures some illness, and you*

18

have discovered it," I kept going. *"You are right, this is a magical herb, and it cures things. I am afraid I will have to disappoint you, and tell you that I didn't discover this. This isn't an ordinary or unordinary herb. Don't tell me you don't know what this is?"* Amel asked shockingly.

"No, I swear, I have never seen this plant. Please don't tell me that this is it? Amel, please don't tell me that you smoke this stupid thing?" Amel looked at me still surprised that I had never tried the grass, and embarrassed at the same time.

"So, all those stories about you being on drugs are true, aren't they? I asked in a shaky voice.

"Amna, please, don't cry. Take a puff of this," he added as he lit up the dried grass. *"Try it, it won't hurt you!!It will only relax you and make you feel like you are in the clouds. It will make you forget the war, the death the blood, the starvation, the emptiness, the loneliness and all other negative feelings. It will give you wings and make you feel like you are in seventh heaven,"* he kept insisting. *"Come on Amna, chill out!!I have been smoking weed for years now, and I am still alive. This isn't deadly. It isn't dangerous. It is not like other drugs. It isn't made out of chemicals, it is pure nature!"*

"Amel, what is wrong with you? What happened to that blond, smart boy, who was into art, drawing and school? What have you done with him?" I asked wiping my tears.

"What do you mean what happened? Who are you to tell me what is right and what is wrong?" he screamed upsettingly.

"It is easy for you to judge me! You aren't stuck in this land of no hope, no future! You live in America, the land of hope and dreams! Your father is still alive, and mine died because of the war!!!They

19

stole him from me!!What am I supposed to do? What kind of future do you think is waiting for me? How can I keep living? How can I find peace and cope with the loss? How can I sleep without nightmares? " Amel kept speaking.

I wanted to say something, but my guilt kept me quiet for some time. He too took a break from talking. I knew in some way he was right, but I still didn't think that the drugs were the way out.

"Amel, listen to me! I know you are struggling. I understand you, I really do. I feel your pain, and I wish I could take half of it from you. Listen, you aren't the only one hurting. We all are. The war had destroyed something inside of us. It left us alive to suffer, but we must stay strong. We must learn to be positive, to go on. Think about people whose lives are more miserable than our own. Think about those orphans who lost all their family members. Don't forget those who witnessed their mothers and sisters raped, urinated on, and beaten to death. Think about all those little boys and girls who saw their family strangled, cut into pieces, burned alive? Imagine how wounded children without legs, arms, hands, fingers, or eyes feel? Should they too turn to drugs? Aren't they in pain? How do you think the thirteen-year old girls impregnated and forced to have and raise babies feel? Should mothers whose infants were shot, butchered in their own arms be on drugs?" I continued questioning him.

"Amel, listen, you are right, my dad is alive. We were lucky to go to the United States of America, and believe me I would give anything to bring Amija (father's brother) Onur back. I must tell you something, so please listen to me. Amija Onur came to me in my dream, a week before we came here. He

spoke to me and asked me to try to talk to you," I said blowing my nose.

Amel looked at me and laughed. *"Heheheheheheh!!!! Hohohohohoh! Hihihihihih! What do you mean he spoke to you? He is dead! Don't you understand!!What kind of drug are you on? Give me some of that"* he said sarcastically. *"I am not on any drugs. I am telling you about my dream."*

Amel looked patiently, throwing the weed on the floor. He said, *"Amna, please do me a favor? Try to talk some sense into my Amel? He is young and he has his whole life in front of him. Amel is a good boy. He has a great heart. I know that he is coping with all of this the best way he can. I know that he has been hanging out with the wrong crowd, and I think there is still hope for him. However, if he continues living like this and holding onto the negative feelings, being in the negative crowd, and doing negative things, he will lead himself to self-destruction. Amna, please tell him about this dream!? Ask him to rethink his actions and to get out while he can?!Now it is only weed, next time, it will be something else, something deadlier!"*

I finished wiping my eyes and blowing my nose. As I looked at Amel, he had a tissue in his hands too. His face was filled with tears, and his blue eyes shined greatly. We looked at each other and ran into each other's arms. For thirty minutes we hugged, and spoke no words.

I remember seeing signs and posters at school, back in Chicago saying, *"Real friends don't let their friends do drugs!* That is the last thing I said to him. A couple of days passed and Amel came to me. He gave me a folded piece of paper and walked away. I sat down. I opened it and I read it. The letter said:

Dear Amna,

     Thank you for the talk. I am sorry if I said anything hurtful to you, and I apologize. I am grateful for your words, and your concern. I know you are right. I know my dad is right too. I am aware that I am on the wrong path, but I feel it might be too late for me to get out. Please forgive me, and try to understand me. There are people suffering more than me. There are people coping and finding other ways to deal with pain. I will keep this in mind, and I will try to change my doings. I can't promise anything. I want you to know that you tried, and did what was right. Now it is time for me to try. Thank you my sister.

Truly,

Amel.

CHAPTER 2:
Bosnia
June, 2001

I kept rereading Amel's letter, trying to reanalyze it over and over. There was so much inside of me that I had to get out of my system. I desperately needed to tell someone how I felt – to open up, to ease my pain. I ran upstairs to my old room that I once shared with my sister back before the war.

The room was filled with gloomy molecules. It resembled very little the room that once used to be mine. The bunk beds that my father made out of wood using his own hands were gone. The study table that he also made for us was also taken by them. There were no shelves on the walls. No books.

I opened all the drawers of an old dresser, and found a pen and some paper. I lied down on my stomach, and started writing without any thinking.

Dear God,

Please have mercy on my family, and all other people who are suffering, and are lost? Please do something for us? Don't let us continue living like this? Please bring some sense, rightness, humanity, sanity, structure, faith and hope back into our lives?

The war has ended. There is no more fighting, at least not by the aggressor. It seems to me that the war hasn't ended completely. It seems that people are at war within. It seems that they are at war with their feelings, with their actions, their reason, their sense, their vision, their hearts and their souls. They have lost themselves, and have been turned into different beings.

I thought that I have changed significantly, but when I look around, I am having a hard time recognizing everyone around me. It seems to me that the atmosphere in Ex-Yugoslavia is filled with negative particles that people inhale daily. Everyone is hurt, confused, afraid, unhappy and lost.

I saw ten-year-old kids smoking cigarettes, drinking, and doing drugs. What happened to the trust, respect, love, and caring for one another? What happened to the dreams, hope and ambitions? What happened to the Bosnia and Herzegovina from before the war? There are no jobs, no opportunities.

What is the point of living if there is nothing to look for? Please, God, bring hope and faith back into our lives, so that we could find all other elements that are lost?

The aggressor has taken not only our loved ones. It took our hope, our dreams. Please help us find the hope!

Before the war, kids respected their parents and other grownups. Why is there all this defiance, disrespect, this anger?

It seems as if people are living day to day, looking forward to nothing; hoping for nothing-- which is the saddest part of all. Why did they kill the hope?

Life without hope is no life at all. It is suffering. Dear God, please bring back the hope, the unity, the togetherness? Please help people find inner peace and heal their pain?

Please help us get rid of the anger, the fear, the pain, the confusion, the selfishness, mistrust, alcohol, drugs, and disrespect. Please, God, have us learn from our past, teach us how to believe, love and live again?

Sincerely,
A Lost Teenager

CHAPTER 3:
Chicago
Fall 1998

Coming to the United States of America as a teenager, not speaking any English at all, and not having anybody in my class who spoke Bosnian were difficult times. However, I had chosen to swim and not sink. Thanks to my yellow Serbo-Croatian-English pocket Dictionary, and my desire to learn English, to be accepted, I learned to communicate in the new language in less than three months. Not only have I learned English, I also picked up a lot of Spanish, enough to communicate.

After a year, I spoke English fluently, but even though I was fluent, I was afraid to raise my hand in class and answer. Back in Bosnia, I was a straight "A" student. I was in Drama Club, Poetry Club, Modeling, and I was very outspoken. Here, unlike back home, I became shy, afraid of being laughed at due to my accent.

The first three months in this country had felt like three months living on another planet. There was so much to be said; so much to be talked about and shared, but the language and cultural barrier shushed it. There were so many things I had to learn in addition to the language. Language was probably the easiest to acquire, but the culture would take time.

Prior to our arrival to Chicago, I had pictured America as the country from Beverly Hills and other American movies. To my surprise, the America that I had seen upon our arrival seemed completely the opposite. We came here as refugees with forty-dollars in our pocket. Interchurch Immigration Agency helped us settle down and adapt. Several years after our arrival, I taught English at the Interfaith. The agency has helped significantly. We had a relative here, my mom's Aunt, so they helped us a lot too. We stayed with Aunt Amira and her family for ten days.

As soon as my dad found a job, we decided to move out. We found housing at a building "owned" by a man from our city, our neighbor. We were informed that this was one of the "safest neighborhoods in the city." Not much did we know.

Back home we didn't have a lot. The only difference with our living conditions now and before was the food. Here, unlike in Bosnia, thanks to the food stamps, we had enough of food. The first day we came to the States, I got sick. I remember getting food poisoning from eating ten bananas, pudding, chocolate, and chips all within a two-hour period.

We moved into an empty, large, one bedroom apartment full of cockroaches. We scrubbed it down, washed the widows, fridge, and oven. We placed two mattresses inside. Mom and dad slept in our living room and Lamija and I got the bedroom.

During the day, we would take the mattresses into our room, and bring them back at night. We bought some posters at a Dollar Store and placed them on our walls. Every morning, as we woke up, we looked at Ricky Martin, Usher, Backstreet Boys, NSYNC, Spice Girls and my favorite of all, Leonardo DiCaprio. I had watched Titanic many times, and each time I cried. DiCaprio became my "dream guy."

We had found an old couch, dirty, ripped in a couple of places and very uncomfortable to sit on. We covered it with a red blanket and hid all of the imperfections. My mother found an old baby-blue rug thrown in the garbage of our alley. She washed it with laundry detergent and a brush, and brought it in to cover the cold hard-wood floors.

Dad found a job and worked as a construction worker at our "friend's" company. After he received his first pay, he took us out to eat at McDonald's, a place we only saw on television commercials' till this day. Since our English was very limited we struggled as we tried to order, *"Please, fries, Coca-Cola, and sandwich"* I said ashamedly." *"Kako se kaze pletina?" (How do you say chicken?)* I asked my folks, hoping that they would know how to say chicken. *"Mogu li vam pomoci?" (May I help you?)* – a friendly man in a Serbian accent approached us, speaking our language.

"Yes, please?!" Four of us answered simultaneously. We came two weeks ago, and our English is "zero" we added in Bosnian.

After we ate, dad took us shopping to Kmart. We needed lots of things. Cousin Jusuf and his family had bought us winter coats. Lamija and I chose the same ones. Both of these coats were double-sided. One side was black, and the other side was silver-metallic. These were the coolest coats we had since the war. They were the first-new things we owned in the longest time.

One time, in Bosnia, while we still lived as refugees in Vranduk, my mom's cousin who escaped to Germany sent us a package. I had never met this cousin before, but I will never forget how happy she made us feel. She sent us a package of clothes and shoes. Some she bought for us from her own pocket.

Other outfits were given to them by the Salvation Army, and donations. There was one dress. It was silver and pink, just above the knees. The dress had a zipper in the back, and matching, silver-pin-striped-shorts. I used to wear this dress only when I would go in public. It was the only—

28

and the best piece of fabric—I owned during the war.

As we got to Kmart, everyone wandered off in a different direction. Lamija couldn't be found for a long time. We found her in the toy aisle, looking at dolls and playing with them. She was twelve at that time. Both she and I had missed out on a lot. During the war, our toys were sticks and pretend-dolls that we made. We never learned to ride a bike—till years later. We never played video games. We never learned to play an instrument. We had no books. I used to make my own books out of old newspapers and yellow stained paper I found in the dumpster. I wrote my own stories and textbooks, and I drew stick figures. We made-up our own stories, and based our play on our "imagination." Lamija's favorite game was *The Next Idol*, and mine was *Play School*.

A month after our arrival, something I have never imagined – happened. It was October, Halloween month, a month of costumes, candy and fun. Lamija's's class did an art project for Halloween. There were two Bosnian students in Lamija's class. Both of them spoke English. On our way home, sister proudly carried her art work. Unlike me who was shy and introverted, Lamija, even though three years younger than me, was very outspoken. She was loud, full of energy and life, not afraid of anything or anyone. She had courage. She wasn't afraid to take risk. As we walked home Lamija made me laugh. Like always, she was cracking jokes and being a comedian. A group of older girls, five or six of them, one being the size of three of me stopped us.

In a high pitched, angry, demanding voice, the tallest and the heaviest one of them yelled; *"Gimme that thing!! Lemme have it white gurl!!!"* Surprised and afraid at the same time, we just looked at them and kept walking. *"Didncha hear what I said you*

29

dummy? Cancha speak any English??? Who do yahl think ya are? Arencaha deaf?" one of the big girls asked forcefully while the others laughed at us.

I have never been a racist. I was raised believing in equality and respect for *all* people. To me there were only two groups of people; good people and bad people. These girls didn't seem to fit into the "good category."

I didn't understand most words she spoke to me. This sounded like some "different English," something that seems to be impossible to learn or understand. I thought, *"Gosh, this is all I needed. It isn't enough that I have to learn not only English and Spanish! Now, I will have to learn this "weird language" too!"* I got the message through her body gestures. We kept walking. We were afraid to look back. Ignoring them made them angrier and louder. They started cursing. *"F... you!!! You st...d a.. b.....!!!Who give ya right to ignore us? Aincha afraid of what might happen to yah if yah don't do what we wanh?" Heyyy lissen to us yah du..... When I'm talkin to yah!!!Give that or else yaahl see!!!"*

I wanted to end this. I hoped to calm them down, and come up with some kind of compromise. I gathered some courage and said in a low-pitched-tone of voice, secretly hoping they wouldn't hear me *"Shut up!"* This only triggered more rage. I had no idea that there were other words that meant the same. "Be quiet" was an unknown phenomenon for me. I've heard "Shut up" from my cousin when she spoke to her kids. I thought it sounded "cool." This was the first English word I learned. I thought I might as well use it. This sure wasn't a smart move. I slowly turned my head and saw how angry they got. Their faces filled with rage and they were ready to explode.

They were ready to do all... Moments later

Lamija and I ran as fast as our little feet could take us – but not fast enough... From behind, unexpectedly a strong punch hit my white and reddish cheeks. "Baaahhhhmmmmmmmm"

As I turned to see the face of the crazed girl, another, even stronger punch came from the left side. I lost my balance. My cheeks were burning and felt as if they were getting numb. Ironically, I was about to have a tooth fixed after school. *This sure beats the injection. Great! It seems as if this time, I will be spared from getting my gums and cheek injected.*" There were stars in front of my eyes. Everything around me became blurry. As I tried to keep my balance and not fall, an adult female voice brought me back.

"Hey you girls stop that!!!Come here!" she yelled. *"What do you think you are doing? Is that how you resolve disputes? Whatever might be the reason, it is just two of them and five of you. Violence is not the answer to problems! Everything could be solved with words! Remember that!"*

A short, hefty lady with brownish and yellowish face said. She had a very noticeable-orange raincoat, and a hat on her head. Surprisingly the five girls were frightened by a woman shorter than them, and her innocent-looking face. In less than two minutes, they were gone. There were no signs, no foot prints of them.

A nice lady approached me. She gave me hug, patted my hair and asked; *"Are you ok sweetie? What happened, tell me. Let's call police and make sure this never happens again."* I looked at her in confusion and shock.

I was afraid of the word police, since I wouldn't be able to tell my side. I simply said, *"I'm Ok."* I took Lamija's hand and kept walking. She tried asking

31

more questions, but decided to give us a break.

Sister and I ran home. We kept turning our heads to see if we were being followed. Our hands and our whole bodies vibrated. Both of us cried.

After we calmed down, we had decided not to do anything since we couldn't speak English nor defend ourselves verbally. Mom said that it was best to let it go. Who knows what would happen if we told someone. They might never leave us alone. We were also afraid that telling someone in school might cause even more harm and put our whole family in danger. After this incident my mom walked us to school back and forth.

CHAPTER 4:
Chicago
1999/2000

One night, the fire woke us up at around midnight. The night of the fire we were awakened by loud banging on the back door. It scared us so much, that we thought the war came again.

"Adem, wake up!" mom yelled. Dad got up startled, not knowing what was happening. It took him moments to get his thoughts together.

Lamija started crying, and asking, *"Mom, dad is the war again?" Are we going be hungry just like before? What about concentration camp? Please don't tell me we will have to go there? I don't want to lose you all!!"* she spoke through tears. *"Lamija, war is over. I promise. Just relax, and stop crying. Let dad open the door to see what is going on,"* mom said calmly. I thought to myself, *"If it isn't war, it sure is a robbery, or a gang activity. This isn't a nice neighborhood. All we need is to get shot now, here. What if those girls have their hands in this?*

There was a lot of resemblance to the war. Something terrible smelled in the air, as if something was burning. *"Who is?"* dad asked in his broken English. *"It is me, John, from upstairs!!There is a fire in the building!! Open up!! Get out of the building!"* one of the twins, with light-brown-skin who resembled our President Barack Obama, yelled.

"One minute please!" dad answered. *"Obucite jakne, i izlazite!"* (Put on your coats, and run out!) Dad ordered us. We put tour coats on, and got out as fast as possible. The fire and the smoke was spreading fast. The police and the fire trucks took me back there...

As we walked to the street, the top floor in the

central building and the one underneath were full of smoke.

"Where are Sonya and Marko? Where are their kids?" mom questioned, as we looked around to see if they were in the crowd. That is when dad ran to the back of the building, upstairs, to see if they were still inside. About ten minutes later, they were out safe and healthy. Dad came to the rescue just in time.

The next day the news people, news trucks and the cameramen came to report the attacks. That night, I was on channel two, five, seven, and nine. A Spanish lady with a microphone came to our door to ask for an interview. Someone in the neighborhood told them that the Bosnian girl spoke Spanish. I refused to speak in Spanish, since I wasn't fluent. They interviewed me for about twenty minutes, but showed only a two minute portion of the interview.

I remembered thinking, *"Great!!I get to be on television. How cool! This might be a chance to get discovered and asked to be a model for some fancy, schmancy modeling agency. I could tell them that I am writing a book about Bosnia. Gosh! I must start writing it in English, if I want to make something out of myself. If this doesn't happen now, I will just model. Everyone says that I could be a model, why not? My dream of being famous might not be so far, after all. I know what I'll do! I will write a book, publish it, and send it to Hollywood. They will ask me to turn it into a movie. Since I am pretty, I could be an actress too! This way I will get it all. I will accomplish my dream of becoming a writer and I will be on television too."*

On the night the interview aired, I remember thinking, *"Great, I came out looking beautiful. My curls look good, and my English sounds pretty good too! Not bad for a fire story after all. I guess in every bad there is good. You just have to find it."*

Not long after the fire, we moved out of the building. Daddy was offered another job. Now that he was going to earn more, we were able to move into a larger apartment, and buy new furniture.

We moved, to what we thought, was a better neighborhood. This building too, was owned by a Bosnian. The apartment was located in an Indian/Pakistani neighborhood.

Our first neighborhood resembled, "Little Mexico" and an "African-American and Mexican Ghetto." This apartment was located in the heart of "Little India" and "Little Pakistan." As you would walk down Devon Avenue, you could hear people speak the same language as the one in Bollywood movies. Even the little girls wore long beautiful yellow, light-blue, pink, purple, orange, red, and white dresses. Everyone dressed colorfully in all spectrums of color. The small shop windows were filled with yellow eighteen-carat-gold necklaces, rings, bracelets, nose jewelry, fancy dresses and traditional Indian and Pakistani outfits. There were lots of restaurants with rich smells, spices and exotic foods. In addition to the restaurants, there were many small beauty shops.

Here you could get your manicures and pedicures, hair colored, styled and cut, eyebrows threaded, colored and waxed, and special occasion make up and henna designs done. Also, this street was full of small electronic stores, quick-marts, Laundromats, perfume-shops and kosher and halal meat markets. You could do all your shopping on this street.

Our new apartment had two bedrooms. It was located on the top floor. The apartment was a lot nicer than the last one. We bought new furniture, and settled down. Our new place looked nice. The only

35

problem with this place was parking. There was no parking. You would have to drive, if you are lucky, at least an hour every day. On the weekends, parking was impossible to find. We learned this only after we moved in.

One day my father took a walk around the neighborhood. He desperately wanted to find a parking spot for our car. He was willing to pay a hundred dollars extra a month, so he decided to look around to see if there was anything being rented. As he walked down the alley, where most garages and private parking spots were located, he passed by an open garage. A bunch of guys were whispering something. In his limited English, he understood the word "drug," but kept walking. As he speed-walked, he wanted to make himself invisible, but it was too late.

The group of multi-racial big men saw him walk by the garage and started running after him. As he turned around, he realized that his crime was being in the wrong place at the wrong time. A forty-year-old man was running from a well-built, long-haired, bearded and tattooed angered twenty-year old holding a knife in his right hand.

Dad ran for more than a mile. The guy after him was only a foot behind. Even though he was younger and in better shape than dad, dad ran fast enough. As he got out of the alley, dad ran inside one of the Arab stores that sold Eastern-European imported groceries.

A Bosnian lady worked at the register. As dad ran in, the twenty-year old gang banger ran inside as well. Tired, shocked and scared, dad shouted in English, *"Please Help!! Call Police!"* The Bosnian lady knew us. We used to buy Podravka, Brother and Sister and other products that we loved from back home. She knew that dad was in trouble, so she called her boss right away.

A short, curly-haired brown-skinned Arab approached the young man who was after my dad. *"Get out of my store before I call police!"* As the gang banger heard the word police, he turned around and ran outside.

Daddy decided that it wasn't safe to get out of the store and go home, in case they were still after him. If they followed him, they would know where we lived. This would bring our entire family in danger. He called a cab and asked the taxi driver to take him to a friend's house. He stayed there for couple of hours, and the friend brought him home. It wasn't long after this incident that we moved to our third apartment. The third apartment was owned by a Croatian guy, and it was in a safer neighborhood.

CHAPTER 5:
Chicago
July 2006

Having survived the war, genocide, concentration camp and starvation, I thought that I left all my traumas and mishaps behind. We came to the United States of America on September 15th, 1998 in hopes of having a better, brighter and safer future. July 12th, 2006 was supposed to be the day when I was going to find out the gender of my baby. I expected this day to be one of the most beautiful and the most exciting days of my life... Once again, life and fate have disappointed me. Instead of finding out the gender of my baby, I found myself stuck underground in the subway of a Metropolitan Beauty, Chicago, in a Blue-line train accident.

Everything happened so fast... I got on the blue train at the UIC/Halsted station. I sat down and ate cherries. Couple of stops later I heard a loud-metal-screechy noise and a burning smell. As the train halted, the red cherries went all over. People jumped out of their seats. They walked over my cherries. They smashed them-- they squeezed them until all blood-like juice came out. The car behind us went off of the rail tracks. The problem was unknown. This was something that nobody expected to occur. Everyone was shocked and frightened. Suddenly, complete darkness appeared, as if the sun had been blocked by the clouds. The lights shut off. People started screaming and yelling for help. *"Help!!! Help!! Please help us! Someone please open this door!!Please save us!!*

I can't breathe!!! Hooohooohooo!!! Mommy, mommy, I am scared!!! Could someone tell us what is going on?!! Does anybody have a telephone signal?

38

Someone call 911!! Mama, please hold me tight. I can't see anything!!Does somebody have a flashlight, a lighter? Que paso? (Spanish: What happened?) Donde esta la luz? (What happened to the lights?) Algien por favor llama la ambulancia!?(Could somebody please call the ambulance?) Abren la puerta!! (Open the door!) Salga nos de aqui?!! (Get us out of here!) I am scared of the dark!!I have asthma, somebody help?!!Please, watch my leg, it is broken!! My baby's pacifier fell down on the floor, someone please pick it up!? I am pregnant, please be careful, don't push me!!!

People kept going simultaneously. I stood motionless and speechless. My body was paralyzed. My brain and thoughts as some kind of hyper molecules had been awakening. I held my abdomen, and tried to see if the baby was moving...

Unlike the rest of the students, mothers, children, businessmen and women, senior citizens, this wasn't my first time facing death. As people screamed, cried, asked for help, I stood silently not uttering any words, not believing what was happening. Inside the cars there was darkness, chaos, panic and smoke. Once in a while someone would turn on their phone for a second to see. They would close it immediately to spare the battery and save it for worse. As I sat and waited, people pushed each other, they coughed and ran outside.

"Please, watch my foot!! Stop pushing me!! Calm down!!Take it easy!! They will come for us!!They will open the door and get us out of here!! Folks relax! Don't panic!!See, the door is open. Don't push each other!" someone from the crowd shouted.

Miraculously, doors opened. I waited for everyone to leave. I was stuck back there... I was afraid of being pushed or hit in my belly, so I chose to be the last one to leave our car.

Just like the inside of the cars, the outside was dark and gloomy. There were infants, pregnant women, preschoolers, elementary school kids, teens, college students, employed males and females and senior citizens, some healthy and others in wheelchairs or walkers. For them this was the scariest experience ever. For me, it was only one of many.

After some waiting in line, we started moving. As we got out, someone from the crowd shouted, *"Take off your jackets, sweaters and hoodies!!Use them to cover your mouths!!Try not to inhale the burning smell!!"*

As we moved slowly, we covered our faces using our sweaters, hoodies, shirts and other clothes, trying not to inhale all the smoke. We moved slowly in a line that seemed to have no end. I coughed. My chest was hurting. My throat felt as if I was coughing out blood and not usual mucus. I couldn't breathe. I felt as if I was being strangled, chocked, and drowned slowly to death. I felt as if I was back there again...

I was nauseous and wanted to vomit. I felt a headache being born. The pain started from the neck, and it spread to all sides of the head. It was the most painful headache I ever felt. My lower back started hurting too. I stared feeling as if it was that time of the month. The baby became quiet. It wasn't moving... My sweat glands and my pores were dilated excessively. Salty mixtures of liquid ran down my entire body. My heart was beating loudly thump-thump-thump-thump. I felt as if it was about to burst out. The only thing I could do now was to pray to God for another chance.

"Dear God, why is this happening to me now, thirteen years after I survived the war, concentration camp and starvation? Why now when I finally have

a reason to live? Dear God, please don't take away my child, my brightness, sunshine and my light? How ironic it is that I might die here, in a country of hope, a country of promise?"

Little had I known that this wouldn't be the last time I would see death.

"What did I do to deserve this? You know I believe in you and pray to you every night! You know that I try to be a good wife, daughter, sister, granddaughter, neighbor, human being and a friend. Why do you keep testing me and bringing me in touch with death? Why do I keep walking through the darkness? Why is the darkness fallowing me everywhere I go? When am I going to get a break? What do I need to do to change my destiny, my fortune my luck? I hate trouble, but trouble seems to be in love with me? Are you punishing me because I told refugees from Sheher, (one of the villages surrounding Zepce that they smelled?) I didn't know those refugees were running for their lives. I didn't know they were forced out of their homes? I didn't know that they came to our basement, where we hid from shells and other explosives, to hide from the aggressor, for 144 hours and 8,640 minutes. I was only nine back then. I didn't mean what I said," I finished sobbingly.

The next dark, scary forty-five minutes was spent thinking about my family, my past, my present and imagining my future. I imagined being in Hawaii with Jaan and our two kids.

We had two gorgeous, energetic and intelligent girls who looked so much alike. They had long, light brown-curly-hair, and looked like both of us. They giggled and smiled all the time. The older one was Hana and the younger one was Sara. We were laughing, running, playing *"Tag-You're It"* They ran

41

and they sang *"If you're happy and you know it clap your hands...!!!* We followed along. On the beautiful sand, there were palm trees all over. The birds were singing, children were making sand castles and digging holes. Mommies and daddies played cards and enjoyed the sun. Many people were surfing, parasailing, riding boats and snorkeling. The older people were relaxing on the beach chairs underneath the colorful umbrellas, reading romance, science-fiction, fiction, and non-fiction books, while they drank colorful-tropical drinks on ice with umbrellas. There was so much happiness at this place, and I felt as If I could spend my entire life there.

I was brought back to the present when someone yelled, *"The firefighters are in the tunnel!! The exit is not far away!! Keep walking!! Soon we will make it out!! Stay strong a little longer!!! Gracias a Dios, vamos a vivir!"(Thanks God, we'll live!)*

I was exhausted, thirsty and sleepy. I had no energy left inside of me whatsoever. I wanted to sleep. My breathing became more difficult than before. I was sweaty and burning hot. I couldn't keep my head up. I became so heavy, and all I wanted was to sleep.

"Are you ok? You don't look too good? Look up! There is not much left! The stairs are close by. That means that the exit is here! Don't give up now!! Keep walking!" a calm, chubby and friendly-looking African American lady, who looked like my Spanish teacher from high school, said.

I turned around and answered, *"I can't go any longer"* as I coughed. It tasted like smoked blood. Yucky! *"I don't want to go. My baby isn't moving. I think she — I can't go on without her. If my baby isn't well, I don't want to be okay either. I don't want to be saved. I don't want to live without her..."* I answered.

"Listen to me! You are going to get out of here! Your baby is okay! She is alive! She is protected in your belly! She will be ok and you will be good too!! Now get yourself together and start moving! We must get out of here as soon as possible," she ordered me.

I wanted her to be correct. I prayed she would be right. I needed her to be true.

"Hey you keep moving!! Stop talking! We want to get out of here!" somebody from the back of the line yelled.

As I wiped off my tears, I covered my face with a light-summer sweater and I moved my feet. Soon we reached the emergency stairs. They looked as if they were barely used. The stairs were a yellowish-orange-like color, and looked a little rotten. The exit couldn't be seen from down there.

As I looked up, the exit seemed to have been miles away, and I didn't know if I would make it. I felt as if everything around me moved. I felt as if everything around me looked double, gloomy and shaky. I pushed myself, and moved up slowly.

After some time, we climbed up the emergency stairs and rays of sun light were visible from the little hole that was our exit. The air smelled fresh and pleasant, but I still had difficulty breathing. I coughed and I wheezed. My eyes were blurry and itchy. They were filled with tears.

A man with stunning white teeth and smile, gave me a hand, and pushed me up. He was dressed in paramedic uniform.

I looked up and saw helicopters. I turned my head right and left, and saw ambulances, news truck, people carried and taken somewhere, paramedics giving oxygen masks, cops, firefighters, bottles of water, people washing the fog and black dirt from their eyes so that they could see and the rest of the citizens watching in shock. It all reminded me of back there...

The friendly-paramedic that gave me a hand handed me an oxygen mask and asked, *"Are you ok? Is there anything about your health that we should know right away? Do you have any pre-existing health conditions that we should know of? I am pregnant, and my baby is not moving. "*

"Don't worry; your baby will be fine! We will take you to the hospital now! Remember, in order for your baby to be fine, we must make sure that you are ok too! Take it easy, and think about how you will feel when you see and hold your baby first time."

I was carried onto the ambulance and taken to one of the hospitals.

CHAPTER 6:
Bosnia
June 24, 1993

Nee-nah nee-nah takka-takka-takka-takka --- rat-a-tat-rat-a-tat — boom...wham--sssshblam...were the sounds that made my ears ache.

The streets of the city of Zepce were filled with bodies and parts of bodies of dead men, women, teenagers, middle-school students, k-4 graders, preschoolers, kindergarteners, toddlers, infants, lost dogs and curious cats, hard-working ants, frightened birds, hungry cows and horses enjoying their last meals. The thunder, the storm and rain of shells and grenades filled the air of a once beautiful city.

Zepce was a small but beautiful city located in Central Bosnia. There were churches, mosques, post office, town hall, schools, pharmacies, hospital, supermarkets, shopping center, flea market, bridges, hills, Movie Theater and a mineral water source that came from ground. It had buildings, houses and rich land planted with lots of fruits and vegetables.

Zepce was inhabited mainly by Christians, Muslims and Orthodox. All three religious groups lived peacefully in harmony for years. One day, the peace and harmony was broken. For me, it all started the day we were forced to hide in our basement. For others, the harmony ended after President Josip Broz Tito's death.

Boys and men, ages fifteen to sixty-five, went to defend us. My cousins, aunts, my grandmother, my sister, mom, my handicapped-uncle, I and some of our neighbors sat quietly in one of the rooms in basement of our house. Fifty of us feared that the cruel and the damn grenade might be thrown at our shelter. We knew that our chances of staying alive, and not hit by a bomb, grenade or a shell were slim. All males old enough to hold hunting guns were on the front line defending us from the aggressor.

If peace was here, most of us would have been in our warm homes. Some of us would have been reading stories, watching, cartoons, movies, making delicious meals, studying, playing games or watching the lottery; hoping and asking God that one of us was a winner in the game of luck. Interestingly, from the hills that surround Zepce, we did look like the tiny balls with numbers engraved on our backs placed inside the vacuum/plastic tube, where one by one we would be exiting whenever our time would come. This time we wouldn't exit as the lucky balls with the numbers people hoped were the winning numbers, but like the balls that prayed to God that they wouldn't be chosen, because those that had the power to choose, didn't have hearts nor morals.

This war to some was indeed an entertainment game. While those that played the game enjoyed themselves, everyone around me, including myself, tried to erase the negative thoughts and to think about something pleasant, like the past...

I was taken back to that time when Santa Claus that resembled daddy, dressed in a red outfit, with red cheeks, white beard, and big glasses, rang our door bell on New Year's Eve. We grew up with New Year's trees that we put up and decorated after Christmas. In addition to the two Eids that we celebrated, my third favorite holiday was New Year's Eve and New Year's Day. On the two Eids, after we kissed our parents, grandparents, uncles, aunts and other relatives, and after we filled our wallets with money, we would go down our street in big groups.

In our religion, we have two major holidays,

46

the two Eids. The first Eid is called Eid Al-Fitr also known Ramadan Eid. Eid Al-Fitr is known is celebrated at the end of the Ramadan, the month of fasting, during which, Muslims give *Zakat*, charity. On that day, *Sarma, Burek, Sirnica, Lukovice, Somun, Begova Corba, Bosanski Lonac, Punyene Paprike* and many other flavorsome traditional dishes are prepared. As for the deserts, pastries, and homemade sweets, *Baklava, Hurmashica, Shampita Rolat, Oblatna, Halwa Kadaif and other homemade pastries that overwhelm your sense of smell and take you into an exotic place are made.*

Even if you fast for thirty days, you cannot lose weight because you gain it all back in that one day. Families get together after men come back from the prayer service. They sit, they eat, drink, talk, laugh, share stories, pray, and enjoy themselves listening to *Sevdah* (traditional music) and dancing *Kolo* (traditional dance).

We used to get presents from Santa Claus on New Year's Day. It made me happy. Getting presents was nice, but getting money was even better. There wasn't a single house that we wouldn't visit and get a coin or a bill from. It's kind of like a combination of a Thanksgiving, Halloween, and a Christmas holiday celebrations in the United States, just better. Instead of treats, you get money on Eids.

Some of our Catholic and Orthodox friends and neighbors participated in the tradition as well. Who wouldn't, especially when getting money is involved? Out of respect for each other, we used to participate in their holidays too. We had to say was *"Bayram-Eid Mubarak Olsum!"* to get money on Eid and kiss the hand of the one who opened the door. We had no trouble doing any one of those two. Some adults didn't even give us their hands to be kissed.

47

The second Eid is called Eid Al-Adha, also known as Kurban Eid which is celebrated after Hajj, the pilgrimage to Mecca. On this day, those who can afford it, buy a lamb or a cow and give meat to their family, friends and neighbors. This Eid is celebrated the same way as the Eid Al-Fitr.

On Easter, we would color eggs, and on the Day of the Dead, we used to jump up the fire with our Croatian friends. Before the war, it didn't matter what religion you followed. We lived with the values of unity, respect and love towards each other. We all believed in one God, we all tried to be good, moral and respectful people, and that was the most important thing. I remember the excitement, the awe and the happiness I felt the day Santa Claus rang our door bell and brought us gifts.

In the midst of my thoughts flying in all directions, my father appeared at the door of the lower-level of our house where we were hiding. This time, he wasn't dressed as Santa Claus. A man, five-feet-eleven inches tall, with light brown curly hair, athletic and muscular body and eyebrows the same color as his hair, thin, but rich as if they have been perfectly done. He had round big eyes as blue as water, which looked different than usual. The color of his eyes, the shine, seemed to have been scared away and the fear dominated them. He didn't look like the same man who once used to enter his cabinet makers or carpenter's shop, humming and singing because he loved what he did for a living. Dad came in with fear, helplessness, hopelessness and the look that told you all...

In a powerless voice, he said, *"I am afraid I have some bad news! The Serbs entered the city. They came in with several tanks with them. It seems like the Croats and the Serbs got together. They*

48

joined their forces. We are left with no choice but to turn ourselves in and become their prisoners, or else death awaits us!"

The reason why the Croats and the Serbs had *united* was obvious; to harm, destroy and erase Bosnjaks (Bosnian Muslims). Why? I don't know? How does a friend, a colleague, a student, a patient, a classmate, a neighbor became an enemy, a killer, a murderer, a rapist, a thief over night?

For many years they went to school with us. They worked with us. We socialized. We celebrated Births, Anniversaries, Weddings, New Years, Christmas, Easters, Eids, Christenings, Sunnet's (Circumcisions) and May Days. We ate from one plate. We bit the same piece of bread, and drank from the same glass.

Now, all was forgotten. Everything was gone. Our togetherness, our respect, our love for one another was lost. Our peace and our trust disappeared.

Why? I wish I knew. The Bosnjaks' soldiers didn't have a choice, or weapons to defend us. All Muslim's living in the city of Zepce, as well as its closest suburbs, except for Preko, which was located on the other side of the Bosna River, had to give up and go to concentration camps.

In Bosnia and Herzegovina, there were many countless and some nameless Concentration camps run by Serbs and Croats, such as Silos, Nova Trgovina, and Perkovichi in Zepce, Omarska, Keraterm, Trnopolje, Manjaca in Prjedor and Kozarac an many more.

Sadly, the Concentration Camps were institutions, worse than prisons, in which one was not only wrongfully convicted and incarcerated, but destroyed. In other words, concentration camps were places whose goals and philosophies were to erase, to destroy all personal, ethnic, national, religious and other values.

Throughout the history of human existence, concentration camps were institutions, in which a person already developed and raised with specific characteristics, religious values, dreams, goals, beliefs, if lucky to survive physically, would become completely transformed; in other words, destroyed. Surrender, in our case was planned to be not only physical and material, but emotional/psychological as well.

It was the ultimate surrender, a relinquishment of possessions and of our home. We had to leave all we had – the house that my mom and dad built from love, so that another can destroy or enjoy. Losing the material thing isn't nor should be painful, but giving up memories, experiences and emotional connections really hurts. It was hard to give up the home in which I've spent my childhood.

I've felt as if I was abandoning and betraying my memories, and ending my childhood. As a matter of fact, the moment when I heard the terrible news that Bosnjak's have lost control, killed my childhood and at the same time gave birth to fear, helplessness, hopelessness, blame, disappointment and disillusionment.

While listening and observing the panic around me, the sense of loss and rape filled me. Even though my body was literally still inside our house, I started missing all the memories that I had experienced in this house in nine years of my life...

As a matter of fact, I remembered coming home the first day from school, filled with excitement and awe. I remembered watching *The Bugs Bunny, The Smurfs, Tom and Jerry, Pink Panther, The Little*

Red Riding Hood, Cinderella, Sleeping Beauty, The Gingerbread Boy, Aladdin and the Wonderful Lamp, Ali Baba and Forty Thieves, Rapunzel, The Ugly Duckling, Pinocchio, Thumbelina, The Bell, Goldilocks and the Three Bears, Puss in Boots, Little Mermaid, Snow White, Hansel and Gretel and others. I remembered coming home from school all in tears because I got my first "C." I remembered my mom going to school to tell my first grade teacher Sofia, who was also my father's teacher to give me an "F" so that I can learn that it's okay not to get straight A's. I am not sure if I ever learned that not getting straight A's is acceptable.

CHAPTER 7:
Bosnia 1993

I didn't see when dad left. The rest of scared women, kids and older men and women started chatting all at once. It became unbearable to listen. My Grandmother Fatima was sobbing in the choir of others. Some refugees kept it to themselves. Others talked to our neighbors. The refugee babies cried as their mothers tried to calm them down by feeding them, bouncing them, and singing lullabies. There was one young lady, in her early twenties with an infant in her arms. She was beautiful, but she looked extremely exhausted and ill. Her baby was so small. Years later, I learned the reason why she cried silently at all times, and why she refused to eat or breast feed her new-born. Back then, I thought she didn't want the baby. I thought she didn't love him enough.

This young girl gave birth to the newborn just three days before they burned her in-laws alive and shot her husband after they raped her in front of him with some sharp metal objects. Her body was sore from child birth, to them it didn't matter. She was bleeding at the time they raped her in front of her husband who couldn't do anything. They didn't care. She and the baby were only alive because Bosnjak soldiers arrived just in time. They shot the cruel men. They "saved her" and the newborn baby boy, or did they? This black-haired pale young girl was only a live because of the baby. While rest of us prayed to stay alive, she did the opposite. She didn't have courage, to take her own life, even though she had thought of it over and over. The baby was the only thing that kept her from taking her life.

I put my two fingers into my ears and I closed my eyes as my tears ran down my cheeks. My curls were messy and extremely oily, since we hadn't brushed or showered for several days. We weren't allowed to go upstairs. It was too dangerous.

Sometimes, one of the adults went up, brought some food and basic needs and came downstairs right away. Our basement wasn't connected with upstairs. It had separate entrance. I kept pushing myself to remember, and remember – so that I could live in the past, so that I could stay being a child. I didn't want to stop recollecting memories, because I didn't want to imagine or experience the cruelties, the pain, the hunger, the trauma or the concentration camp that everyone in the crowd kept talking of. As a matter of fact, I tried separating and isolating myself from the chaos. A nine year old child isn't expected to react with shock, or to fully understand the meaning of concentration camp, but I did as soon as we got there.

For me, war started the moment we had to say "goodbye to dad" – just before they took us to different concentration camps. My sequence of memories was broken when I heard my mom beg my father not to burn our house.

"Adem, I am begging you please don't do this?! I understand the emotions that are inside of you. I understand your frustration, fear and anger. For God's sake, don't burn the house that we've built with love, and hard work. Don't do it for the sake of our love and our children..." mom said pleadingly.

She had been a woman with a heart the size of a mountain, filled with love and understanding for everyone; ready to show sympathy, kindness, smile, a hand to all.

She had been ready to stand up and defend even those who hurt her, those who belittled her, offended her. Mom believed in goodness and humanity. She believed that everyone had good

53

intentions, and she believed that everyone had goodness hidden inside.

Mom had been a person whose only arguments with my father were because she would try to stand up and justify everybody. Mama's heart had been full of forgiveness, compassion, understanding, sympathy, purity and innocence. She had a resemblance to Mother Theresa, and that was perhaps her only weakness.

This five-feet-five inch, tall woman, with dark brown hair and eyes slightly darker than her hair, and a complexion that many go to tanning salons to get, was given to her at birth. She had always been on a chubby side, but she never had problems with her confidence and self-esteem. She had been content and grateful with what she was given, and she always smiled. Grandma named her Sabira. Mama had been full of love, passion, positivity and patience.

When I was little, every time my mom talked to me, played with me, and laughed with me, the entire neighborhood knew. She has been open, loud, and full of love. Everyone loved her. She had been a great listener and a friend. Mom had been brought into this world and given a body that resembled her organ of passion, optimism, sacrifice and strength. She had been an excellent cook, baker, a mother, a wife, a daughter, a sister, a daughter-in-law, a neighbor and a friend.

The moment we heard that we must leave our homes and go to concentration camp was filled with father's realism, disappointment and mother's optimism faith and endurance. Dad's movement, his gestures showed only frustration and defeat. At that time I didn't understand why he wanted to burn our home, the same house that he gave lots of energy, sweat and love into. He couldn't stand the thought of knowing that others would destroy it, burn it, or enjoy his souvenir and pride. Half an hour later, we left our loving home, our car and all of our belongings with a blanket, some cans of food and a bag of clothes.

Just across the street from our house, a tall, breath-taking girl in her teenage years was crying. She was having an argument with her mother. *"But, mom, why can't I take my make up with me? It took me six months to save to buy this newest collection of eye shadows, mascaras, lipsticks, eyeliners, and nail polish. Please mommy, let me keep this?"* she begged.

"Jasmina, honey, I told you this already. You can't take make up with you. I promise, once this misunderstanding is over, I will buy you a new better make up."

I looked at them and asked mom, *"What in the world is wrong with them?! Why are they throwing make up?"* I asked.

Before getting an answer to my question, I ran across the street to pick up the make-up. *"Amna!!!Stop!!!Don't touch that!"* mom yelled. I have never seen more make up until that day. I was so tempted to take it and make it mine.

"Amna, sweetie, we are going to a place where having make up can be dangerous for a young lady" mom explained. *Why? Mom? I don't understand?"* I asked.

"You don't have to understand, at this time. I need you to trust me on this. I need you to promise me that this conversation will end here," mom ordered me. It did not take long to understand why being a beautiful young girl in that awful place was bad.

As we were living Berek (our neighborhood) behind, I kept looking up to see if I would see a sign that everything would be fine. Our part of city was known as Berek. It was located just off the highway, very close to the train station, and the soccer field. Every year, each fall, Zepce would held *Vasher* (Carnival) where people from all over Bosnia and Yugoslavia came--there were joy rides, games, live music, roller coasters, toys, sugar candy, entertainers, clowns, souvenirs, and much more.

During this time, the city was lively brimful with joy. Adults laughed, drank, played games, bought gifts for their children. Little boys and girls rode roller coasters, they ran, laughed, and ate ice cream, watermelon cotton candy and celebrated life.

Sadly, the sound of explosives and the sirens indicated the opposite. I didn't know a lot about religion, but I knew that there was going to be a Judgment Day. I felt that this was it. We were ordered to stay silent, and still, as we walked in lines and rows as herds of domestic animals. Walking toward the concentration camp felt like the end of world, that I was responsible for somehow, because I told the refugees from Seher (neighboring village) that they smelled. As a matter of fact, just two days before we surrendered, June 22nd, of 1993, I acted unreasonably and selfishly when I told my mom that the traumatized, tired and hungry refugees from Seher smelled.

Not long after about dozen of strange women and children arrived into our basement, I innocently questioned mother, *"Mom, why do these people smell bad? Don't they have deodorants or perfume?"*

Mom wasn't someone who gets easily angry, but this made her snap. *"How could you ask such a question? Don't you realize they lost everything they had? Don't you know that they ran to escape death? Croats entered their village. They've killed their loved ones. They burned their homes and took away everything that they had. Don't ever judge someone by their looks! You are smarter than that. I taught you better"* mama explained.

Even though I was a child who wasn't completely aware of everything that was happening around me, I did believe that making that comment angered God and transformed me from a child into an adult in only two days.

As we were getting closer to the Hangars, I kept looking for logical solutions, answers, signs, and voices, but I couldn't see any. Something that I did see for the first time in my life, were the eight enormous-looking Serbian tanks.

They only confirmed the inevitable. These man-made objects of destruction moved as if they were ancient rulers everyone feared not to anger or disrespect. As soon as we arrived to the gates of the concentration camp, we were told to form two lines; one for men and the other for women, children and seniors.

I'll never forget the moment when they took away our father from us. I can still feel the pain in my chest — in my throat — the feeling of being strangled — the sob and the fear throughout my body. One of the Croatian soldiers whose face I have completely erased from my mind — violently grabbed my father — and pulled him away from us with a force.

For the first time in my life I saw my dad fight his inner emotions by trying not to let a single tear slip out of his small blue eyes — just like he didn't succeed at liberating us from them – he lost again –
But this time he lost a battle with his emotions. He wanted to, and he tried to say something to us, perhaps to assure us that everything would be okay, but he couldn't.

It seemed as if his voice and his ability to

speak, just like human kind had deserted him. Those that tried to beg, those that knelt on their knees and looked into eyes of some of their fellow classmates, some of their crushes, some of their co-workers, bosses, employees, some of their students, their customers, clients, doctors, apprentices, helpers, were spit on, cursed, slapped, beaten to death or simply ignored.

Just two rows behind us, we heard a conversation between a little boy with blond hair and dark brown eyes and one of the soldiers. It appeared as if Adis wasn't afraid to look at this man directly into his eyes, hoping to get some kind of sign of guilt, recognition and help.

"Mr. Ivan! This is me, Adis, your kumche (godson)! You cut my hair on my first birthday. This is the gold necklace that you bought me as a gift. I still remember when you told me that if anything was ever to happen to mama and tata (dad) you would take me, and would treat me as one of your own. Pleaseeeeeeeeeeee!!! Mr. Ivan, Please help us, please tell these men to let us go back home?! Please tell me that this is all only a bad dream?! Tell me that this is not happening? Aren't you going to say anything? Aren't you going to do something? If your Ivana was in my shoes and my dad in yours, my dad wouldn't let them take her..." the little boy cried as he knelt down on his knees, and held the necklace.

Another soldier forcefully took off Adis's necklace and said, *"Now! Everybody listen up! Remove all rings, bracelets, necklaces, watches and other valuables that you have on you! Those of you who try to hide any of the valuables will face death! Now get going! Turn everything in!"* he shouted.

Mr. Ivan couldn't bear to stay silent. All he said to Adis was, *"Poor child, you must have mistaken me for someone else. My name is not Ivan and I have never seen you or your family. Stop harassing me and just go, there is nobody who can help any of you now"* Ivan added. Adis's neck was bleeding. He sobbed as his body trembled and vibrated. His mother was on the floor. Ivan was out of sight.

As dad was being taken away — he gave us a look that told us that even though we were defeated in every way, and even though they took away everything we had, they didn't rob, nor could they ever rob, the love we had for one another.

The Serb and Croat soldiers carried bags and buckets of golden, pearl, sapphire, emerald, and diamond rings, bracelets, necklaces, earrings, as they happily sang and carried their large rifles.

CHAPTER 8:
Bosnia
June 1993

Our eyes didn't want to part; my eyes stared at my father and on the soldier pulling him forcefully until I lost him in the crowd of fathers, sons, brothers and grandfathers that were being taken to another location.

A young woman with red hair, freckles, beautiful green eyes and long eyelashes caught my eye. She was dressed in a long gypsy-colorful skirt and short sleeve-black shirt with a white pullover. Her face was pale, red, and swollen. Tears ran down her face toward the ground.

Another, older woman, who appeared to be her relative, held her strongly, and tried to shush her. The older woman had a hijab, Muslim scarf, and wore long brown shirt and a matching skirt that went down to her toes.

The young girl spoke through tears to a man being taken away by one of the soldiers. She yelled, *"Amar, my one and only love, please don't leave me?! We just got married last week. What about our honeymoon? You promised, you would take me some place far from here! Please don't leave me!? I love you Amar! If they hurt you, I will take my own life, I swear! I won't be able to go on living without you!"* She said as she knelt down on her knees.

"Lala, please don't cry! Please, don't say these things to me! I love you too, more than anything. I promise you that after I get out, I will take you on our honeymoon. You must promise me that you will stay strong. If anything happens to me, please promise me that you will live!" Amar added as he pushed the soldier away and tried to run to his young

60

wife's arms. Lala was up running towards him too.

That is when both of them were stopped. An older soldier, in his fifties held a rifle on Lala's head. Another soldier took his rifle and with it kept hitting young Amar over and over.

I saw the first five hits that Amar got. He stayed silent throughout the whole maltreatment. There was so much blood on his body and on the cement. Lala was held by three men, and forced to watch as they covered her mouth. What happened next, I didn't see. All I heard were the soldiers yelling as they laughed, *"You s....d Muslim loser! Don't you worry about giving her a honeymoon! We will take care of it! Instead of being pleased by just you, she will be pleased by an army of us! Hahahahaah!"* I had no idea what those words meant. At first I secretly hoped that they wouldn't harm her.

My mother took us to the front of the line where we were about to be searched. We asked no questions. We spoke none of this. That night, I dreamt that Lala and Amar were some place far away from this chaos.

They were together, but they were not happy. He was in a wheelchair. He sat quietly meditating. She kept walking back and forth, humming some gibberish words, moving her head back and forth and holding her belly with her both left and right hands. I was awakened by voices of young girls, begging, screaming pleading to be left alone, to be spared...

Prior to entering the "gates of chaos" they searched us. A twenty-year old male with a friendly face dressed in camouflaged uniform with a deep voice ordered us, *"Put your hands in the air!"* as he pointed at us with his scary rifle. We did as we were told. Another soldier, in his mid-forties used his hands and touched us from our heads to our toes. I looked at mom frightened and embarrassed, not uttering any words, hoping that this would be over with soon. Then we were ordered in a bossier and angrier voice, *"Empty your pockets and bags! Take everything out! Now! Fast! Get moving!"* I felt very afraid, but I said nothing.

We opened our bags and took everything out. Our hands were shaking. Our hearts were beating so fast as if they were on a race. They looked through our pants, shirts, underwear, towels and cans of food, bread, jam, soap, shampoo, bologna, cheese, and photo albums. They were checking for weapons, gold, money or any other valuables or objects that we could use to "harm" them.

My mom had brought a kitchen knife to cut bread. As soon as they found the knife, they threw it away on a pile of other knives, nail cutters and tweezers. Soon they let us in.

We entered the enclosed area filled with numerous people – all lost, sobbing, shaking and talking indistinctively. The place was overcrowded. I don't know the exact number of people that were imprisoned, but in my eyes, there were many.

Why did we end up in this scary place? I didn't know. I still don't know. Is it because we were Muslims? Is it because our people didn't believe that their neighbors and friends would betray them?-- probably.

We were imprisoned by the Old Hangars, a place I haven't visited before this day. Until this day, I had no idea it existed. Old Hangars were located not far from *Charshiya* (Center) with the *Bosna River* running next to it. The elementary school that I attended wasn't far either. Men, on the other hand were imprisoned in couple of different locations. Where they took my father, I didn't know? Would I ever see him again? I hoped and prayed.

My mom tried to find an available space for us to settle down inside the barracks or hangars, the metal storages that people once used to store corn and other crops for winter in. Unfortunately, she had no luck finding shelter for us inside the barracks. Like many other Bosnjaks including our closest relatives, we were forced to settle down outside under an open sky. My mom had brought two blankets with her, so we put one blanket on the ground and saved the other one for the night to cover ourselves. Just a foot next to us, another family settled down, and another – until there was no space left either inside or outside.

As we sat down, Lamija started questioning mom, *"Mama, why are we here? Are we going to sleep here on this hard cement? Why can't we go home? Are they going to shoot us all, like they did in that movie? Are they going to throw our bodies in that big hole, and bury us there? Why is this happening mom? What did we do? Where did they take dad? Are they going to hurt him? Mama, I am scared. I don't want us to die! I don't want to be here. Let's go home!"*

Lamija finished as mom looked at her helplessly, thinking what to say. *"My baby, I wish we go home too. Don't worry, we will be fine. We are not going to be killed. Those things only happen in movies. Not in real life. This is just temporary. Soon we will be released. Soon we will be free. Now I need you too to stay quiet. Don't ask too many questions. Play with your teddies quietly"* mom answered, trying to convince herself that all will be alright.

As night was approaching, the fear was born; the fear of unknown-scary word "rape." We feared of being killed, gassed, beaten and separated during

63

sleep. We were afraid of closing our eyes and not waking ever again. We were worried of closing our eyes and finding our loved ones killed, tortured, taken away.

As night arrived, I wondered how God, the sky, the moon and the stars watched, but did nothing. That night was one of the longest nights ever. The fear, confusion, cold, and the screams of young girls who were taken away did not allow me to sleep.

Before the war, we would go to sleep at 7:30 PM after cartoons and a story time. Now, there was no curfew, no story time. All you could hear was loud music, the drunken soldiers dancing and singing, gun shots every now and then, female voices screaming, begging, and calling for help – some asking to be spared. Others begging to be killed and freed from suffering, mothers hitting their heads, screaming, cursing, some comforting others, some praying to God, and most crying quietly trying to stay invisible.

I hugged my teddy that I got as a birthday present. I held my sister's and my mom's hands, then I covered my face with a blanket trying to hide, trying to disappear or become invisible.

That is when I heard a voice soft as of a child scream. Her voice told me that she couldn't be much older than me, *"Please, don't take me away?! Please don't hurt me?! I am just a little girl? Why are you touching me?! Please take your hands off of me mister? Don't take my shirt off! What did I do?!Please!? Pleeaaasse? Mommy!! Mommy!! Daddy!!! Anybody! Help!!"* she kept going, but I couldn't keep listening not another second. I didn't want to listen. I put my fingers in my ears and I hummed... Sister was asleep. Mom was awake, but she pretended to be asleep.

This was more than enough. I have no idea

when I fell asleep, but not soon after I dozed off I heard women whispering about last night. *"Were you able to sleep? Did you hear the cries, the shootings last night? Who were the little girls and women being taken?"* they kept going.

As soon as I opened my eyes, I checked to see if my mom and sister were next to me. *Amna, did you sleep well last night? What about you Lamija?"* mama asked. *"Mama, what does being raped mean?"* I asked. *"Where did you get that from?"* mom questioned in shock and embarrassment. *"Everyone keeps repeating that word. I don't know what it means."* I explained innocently. *"How can I explain this to you? Hmmm? "* mom passed as she tried to find the right words. *"Well...rape is a very evil thing. It is very immoral, very inhumane. It is something that is wrong, and should never happen. Rape is when wicked men do very ruthless things to young girls, moms, and grandmothers and their private parts. That is all I can tell you now. Don't think about this anymore. Now let's go to that line and get our food!"* Mom finished with a deep sigh.

I just looked down feeling more confused and frightened than before. I remember thinking why would anyone want to harm your private parts? Later I heard that in other concentration camps throughout ia, girls as young as me were raped. Lamija was only six when the war started. I am three years older than sis, but I still remember the day when she was born. It was January 11th, 1987.

As I watched her, I remembered the day she was born. Mommy was coming home with a baby sister. I wanted to surprise them, to do something nice. I decided to ask Nina, our neighbor to go with me to Mrs. Sofia's garden, our Croatian neighbor, to pick flowers for my mom and my sister. That day was the first time I asked permission to pick flowers. Prior to that day, I had a reputation of a "flower thief." I used to steal flowers from neighbors' gardens.

Seeing my sister for the first time was one of the happiest memories for me. She looked so small, so cute, just like a doll that I used to play with. She was tiny, bald, and dark. I had to wait some time to hold her.

Even before my mom came back home from the hospital, I decided that my sister would be named Lamija. I was the first child in my family. I knew that I would no longer be the only one to get my parents' attention and love.

Deep inside, I was afraid that this new baby would be better than me. I was afraid she would be more loved than me, so I tried to behave. I decided that stealing flowers wasn't going to make me more favored.

She was named after a tall, slim, pretty girl that I admired. I don't remember her face because I was only three when my sister was born, but somehow I fell in love with that name. Even though my parents had other names in mind, they decided to let me name my sister.

My little newborn sister became Lamija, just like I wanted. Watching her, this tiny, innocent, skinny little girl with the eyes of honey and the brightness of the sun, I felt sorry for her. She was only six when the war started. She didn't get an opportunity to run around the neighborhood, to climb trees, play hide and seek, play with dolls, jump, run, pretend, read, imagine, go to school ... all of that was stolen from her.

When I was a child I enjoyed my childhood, and did experience those precious, crucial and necessary events in a child's life. Watching her, all those memories became painted vividly in front of me and I wanted to relive them – bring them back to life. I wanted to relive those thoughts, experiences, feelings, joy, and excitement not alone, but with Lamija in them.

The reality made it impossible. Unfortunately, all my hopes and wishes were far from becoming real. There was a clear indication that sis would never get an opportunity to pick flowers from Mrs. Sofia's garden, just like I did the day she was born.

From that day, she and I would have to rely on our imagination; we would have to use sticks, dirt and water to make pretend-dolls. We would have to eat grass to satisfy our hunger, and ride branches of trees as bikes, learn in schools without books, notebooks, pencils, and study with fear of being bombarded and killed...

"Amna, Lamija, eat your food. I want you to eat and to stay strong and healthy." my mom said. The next night and the next eight nights were a "little bit better" because we slept inside one of the barracks.

The second day passed without any major incidents except for several ladies that threw up and got stomach flu. We woke up. We went to get our food and out water.

Since we had to wait for a long time in lines, time went by quickly. After we ate, we talked to our family members, our neighbors and our friends.

I had my collection of fairy tales with me and I read them over and over. Each time I read them, I role-played them and I pretended to be in the fairy land myself as an escape from that awful place.

I wanted to keep a journal, but I didn't know where to start. I was also afraid to open up. What if they searched us again? What if they found it and read what I wrote? I imagined being hanged. I imagined being forced to wear a scarlet letter, being labeled and made an example of. I wanted to become like Ann Frank. I wanted to be just like Ellie Wiesel and I wanted to keep a diary like Zlata—but I was afraid. I was afraid not for my own life. I was afraid that they would hurt sister, mom, dad, and the rest of my family members if they found out what I really thought about them. Writing was just too risky.

CHAPTER 9:
Bosnia
June 1993

On the third morning, we woke up a little later. As a result, our waiting in line turned from an hour to two and a half hours. My mom didn't want to wake us up since this was the first night we slept "ok." We knew that our chance of getting a decent portion of meal was slight — at least, we had no nightmares previous evening.

As we entered the line a woman with a belly and a daughter came right after us. The girl was very beautiful, but very thin. She was tall as me, and she must have been my age. The girl had no hair. Her hair was shaved. She was dressed like a boy. Her mother physically pushed her into the line holding her hand tightly and saying, *"Come here, and don't do this to me! Please listen to me?! You must eat or else you will die!"*

The girl responded with an attitude, *"I don't care if I die! Why would I want to live? I rather die from starvation, than to be killed by them! Look at me? I look like a boy? Look at you mom? You cry every single night – ever since they did that to you! You are not the mother I knew! They stole my mother from me!"* she paused as she cried. *"Shhhhhh!! Larisa! Don't make a scene now!"*

The mother said as she hugged her daughter lovingly. We just listened quietly. *"Mama, Mammy, why did they shoot daddy? How are we going to live without him? Who is going to take care of us mom?"* Both of them sobbed.

The soldiers were couple of lines in front, so they didn't see this. That is when a shot gun was fired. We all went down to the ground covering our heads.

The rest of the waiting in line we stood quietly. By the time we got our food, we lost our appetite, but we ate regardless.

I kept looking if I could see the girl from the line. I wanted to get to know her. I wanted to talk to her. She needed a friend, but I needed one too. The crowd made it impossible. Our concentration camp was gated. It had tall metal fences that were difficult to climb. The edges of the fence were extremely sharp, which made the escape impossible. There were guards and dogs guarding the fence from all sides.

On the fourth day, a woman in her seventies, dressed nicely, and stylishly who used to work as a nurse before the war received the terrifying news. Her name was Salima, at least that is what they called her by. She slept inside our hangar, in a corner, just across our little "bed." Salima seemed calm, faithful and very religious. She didn't wear hijab, but she prayed five times a day, whenever she got a chance.

Even though she was in her seventies she took care of her looks, and had very few wrinkles. Her hair was dyed in ash blond. There wasn't a single gray hair that you could see.

When she spoke she spoke beautifully, intelligently calmly. You could listen to her days and nights, and you wouldn't get bored. When Mrs. Salima spoke, she always said, "Mash-Allah" meaning thank God and "Alhamdulillah" also meaning the same.

She was the one that gave other women and children words of wisdom, hope, faith and peace. She is the one who helped us fall asleep – the one who was there to listen, to give a hug and a shoulder to cry on.

Just after the sunset, after we ate and went back into our hangars, the women started shushing and whispering simultaneously as they looked with pity at Salima. She was finishing her prayers, *"...We-leh-ddaah-leen-Aah-meen."* Then, she gently touched her face with her both hands and got up. She took a thick book and started reading from as her upper and lower lips touched. She knew that all eyes were on her, but she continued reading silently, as if she was aware that something wasn't right. She had a feeling. Everyone did. That day she kept it to herself. She spoke very little. The rest of the evening she continued reading and praying and speaking to nobody. After this day she wasn't the same Salima as before.

We heard that her three sons and her husband were all beaten to death. Nobody knew why. Some say they beat them to death while they prayed. Others say it was because they refused to eat pork. The true reason and way these three men were murdered is unknown. In just five days, Mrs. Salima's gray started showing, her wrinkles became thick, her red cheeks became colorless, her smile was gone – her faith, her optimism and her old self evaporated with her husband and sons. Her body was alive, but her soul passed away. The day, Mrs. Salima lost her family, the rest of us lost too.

On the fifth morning, as we were waiting in food lines, sis with curiosity asked; *"Mom, how come we have to wait for hours to get our food? I miss your cooking mom! Why does my belly make noise? Why am I always hungry and thirsty? Mom, am I going to have a headache again?"*

"Dear Lamija, please try not to attract attention to us, we'll talk about this some other time, now stay quiet because we don't want to get in more trouble, ok sweetie."

She kept going, *"But mom, why are those men always watching us, and pointing their weapons at*

71

*us? Why can't they let us eat in peace?   Mom I'm
thirsty, it is hot, and I want some water..."*

At the same time there was another little girl
having a similar conversation, just few steps in front
of us. She had beautiful golden curls, and eyes as
green as the grass, *"Mama, can we eat something
good this time? I don't want to eat that food that
makes my stomach sick? It is so hard, and yucky?
Mom, how come we can't have any mashed potatoes,
with meatballs or chicken? Maybe if we stay here for
my birthday, they might give us cake?! They will, I
know! I've been a good girl, which is why I know I
will get cake, and maybe even some mashed potatoes
and meatballs."*

*"Dana, please try to stay quiet, we'll talk about
your birthday some other time."* Dana's mom tried to
keep her four-year-old daughter from asking more.

*"Hey you, little Balija (derogatory term for a
Bosnian Muslim), shut a hell up!!!* One of the soldiers
overheard them. With a face as red as chili pepper,
eyebrows lowered to the max, unevenly positioned
yellow teeth, and a breath with an odor so strong that
the smell traveled from his mouth into yours, and
made you want to gag, made you want to throw up,
screamed.

Just before he pushed little Dana away, he took
one of her curls in his monstrous huge hands—

With a cigarette lighter he burned off a big
piece off of her beautiful hair. Dana was in shock.
She didn't cry. She didn't move. She said no words.
Her pupils were dilated and her eyes didn't blink...
Dana's mama pushed him and hit him as hard as she
could using her hand. He took his gun and he hit her
head with it—then he yelled, *"If you say one more
word, I'll make sure that you don't get to be here for
your birthday! I'll shave your head and make*

meatballs out of you! Then I will feed you to the rest of you f..... Balijas. And you..." he turned towards Dana's mom and said, "Teach your child to keep her mouth shut or else I will!!! What the h... you think this is? A hotel? This is not a goddamn hotel where rich breakfasts, big delicious lunches and even bigger dinners are served! This is not a place that throws birthday parties where you get to blow candles and make a wish! The only b..... that is done here is the one we do, and the one we order you to do!!Ok, here, you dirty Baliye will eat anything and everything, even if we decide to feed you shit, even if we ask you to eat the meat of each other!!! So shut your goddamn mouths before I shut them for you!!" the angry, ready-to do all man said.

If it wasn't for another guard, a young man about eighteen years old, with a pleasant looking face, who knows what this monster would have pulled.

"Hey, dude, chill out, and take it easy! Take a sip of this cognac? Can't you see that she is only three or four? Even though she is a Muslim, she doesn't deserve to be talked to like that. Don't you want to have kids one day yourself, dude?"

This only made the first guard angrier. He took the bottle of cognac, and smashed it on the ground. The liquor ran down the cement, and the glass was all over. Then he took out his gun and pointed it not on little Dana, but on his own kind. As he was passing by, another soldier, that was dressed differently, the one that looked like he was of a higher rank came and ordered the one pointing the gun to stop.

"Stop this f....... nonsense! We are not here to hurt our own, so both of you cut it off! Cut it off now!!" the one in charge ordered.

That is when he took both of their guns and sent another two guards to watch us. What happened

73

afterward, I never found out; all I know is that day the food made my stomach feel sick, and made me go to the bathroom, the area designated as restrooms behind the barracks. We ate not to fulfill this need but only to stay alive. A lot of elderly, weak and kids got sick in the concentration camp, but luckily not one of my relatives became too sick.

CHAPTER 10:
Bosnia
June 1993

One day, the Croats cut off our water supply. Ironically, it happened on the hottest day of the summer. I don't recall the exact temperature. The smell that day was unbearable.

Everywhere you turned, the sweat was strong. For days, we didn't shower, and the hot temperature and humidity didn't help at all. The children cried so much that day. Everyone was annoyed, impatient and moody. We were told that they were working on "fixing the water pipe." People were vomiting on their blankets, others, were throwing up behind the hangars — everyone was dehydrated. Since, the water "wasn't fixed" we were allowed to bring water from Bosna River .

The Bosna River is the third longest river in Bosnia and Herzegovina. Its source is at the foothills of Mount Igman at the outskirts of Sarajevo, the capital of Bosnia and Herzegovina. Bosna River runs for 168 miles through Central Bosnia and Herzegovina. It passes through Sarajevo Canton, Zenica-Doboj Canton, and Posavina Canton. Zepce is located in Zenica-Doboj Canton. A canton is small administrative division in a country that is generally smaller counties, or provinces.

The Bosna River, like other rivers throughout the country, was filled with dead corpses. Many Muslim children, women, men and older people were shot and thrown into rivers. There were also those that tried to swim to safer territories and were gunned, bombed, or simply drowned. Many innocent lives tried to run across bridges when they were shot, burned – their corpses ended up in rivers. On that humid, unforgettable day, we were forced to drink water from a river filled with corpses and parts of killed Muslim babies, children, women and men. Years later, my mom told me why the water tasted yucky. We were not forced to eat meat of our loved ones – we did drink water contaminated with human blood...

The water that we drank wasn't ordinary, bottled, purified or filtered water that you normally drink at home. It didn't come from natural or mineral springs. This water was of a special kind, it was flavored water, but not strawberry, cherry, lemon, lime, citrus or any other fruit-flavored. This flavor was exotic; it was the flavor of blood, rotten heads, fingers, toes, ears, stomachs, intestines, hearts and other parts of human and animal bodies. We kids had no idea that this water was of that sort, until later on. Some of us suspected and asked our parents why the water had a weird taste, but were told that it was only our imaginations.

To an exhausted, frightened, weak, hungry and thirsty human who was thrown out of his own home and robbed of freedom, family, privacy and the normal life, anything that can be used to relieve thirst or hunger tastes good. Bathrooms, showers, and baths were only dreams—they didn't exist in our concentration camp. We had to urinate and poop behind the hangars, in public, in front of the whole world.

This was very embarrassing, especially since the senior men were also imprisoned with women and kids. The worst part was trying not to step in stool, since we had no water or paper to clean it off with. Later on, finding a clean piece of ground or grass became impossible — so piles and levels of stool started appearing. The fact that we ate little, kind of helped, since we didn't have to go to the bathroom regularly.

The first day in the concentration camp after we found our "new home," a corner on the concrete, and placed our blanket, I had an urge to urinate. As a child, even before the war, I was an occasion night-time bed-wetter, something that made me uncomfortable and embarrassed. I had a problem, and my problem became more obvious when I would sleep over at my cousins' houses.

Being shot, beaten or raped, even though at that time I had no idea what rape meant, weren't my only fears. I also had my own private little fear, that more than anything, I wanted to hide. I wanted to keep a secret.

It was the fear of peeing and wetting one of the couple of outfits that we could bring with us. It was also the fear of wetting one of the two blankets that we brought. Perhaps the biggest fear related to this problem was letting almost the whole city find out that even though I was nine, I peed on myself at night. I don't recall if I had one of these accidents that night.

After the routine inspection and interrogation, and after we made our "new nests," I said to my mom, *"Mama, I need to pee, where is the bathroom?"*

"Amna, there are no bathrooms here my dear, but I will show you where you could pee. I will take you and your sister together because I am afraid of letting you go by yourself. You never know what could happen."

"But mom, if it is one of those outside bathrooms— where you have to stand on your feet and pretend you are sitting—I don't want to go. Those bathrooms smell."

"Dear Amna, if that was an option I think you'd love it, comparing to what you are about to

see. Here, my children, we must forget about shame, we must not be afraid of "sharing bathrooms" with other little girls like you, other moms, and sick old nanas (grannies) and dido's (grandpas). More importantly, we must be very careful when we walk, so that we don't step in poop or pee, because if we do, there is no water to wash it off. There is no toilet paper either. "

I knew my mother felt bad about us not having bathrooms. I also knew that I had to accept the reality no matter how disgusting, uncomforting or bad it could be. I knew I couldn't use my persuasion techniques because there was nothing you could do to change it. In addition to being a bed wetter, I was also one of those kids that had to pee a lot, one of those that had an urge to urinate (more psychological than physical) about four times in one hour. I also knew that this would be a problem. Since there was so much tension, so much fear and negative energy in the air, I had felt the urgency to go even more.

The very first time my mother took us to "the bathroom" I remember thinking, *"Why can't I pee alone in private? Why are there so many people peeing openly? Why do we have to pee at all?"* As I was taking my little pants off as slowly as I could, Lamija and mom stood in front, using their bodies to shield me.

That is when we saw a woman whose head was covered with a scarf. She wore *dimiye*, a long traditional Bosnian dress. She had the face of someone who has suffered so much even prior to this chaos. She looked like someone who had lost not only one, but many of her loved ones. As she walked, she pushed a man in a wheelchair. The old, handicapped man seemed to have been her grandfather. As she moved her feet slowly, one by one, she imitated movements of someone who sleep-walks, someone whose body is moving, but his awareness and brain is in a state of deep sleep. The man, the grandfather whose wrinkles and baldness shaky hands, told that he could be in his eighties, saluted us saying, *"As-Salamu-Alaykum!"*

"Don't mind me. There is no reason to be ashamed. I look at you as my own daughters, so please don't mind me. ""Wa-Alay-kumu-s-salam grandfather. Don't you worry about us, we will be fine" my mother answered.

I pulled up my pants, and we walked as fast as we could. We were uncomfortable. We also knew that the poor old man felt embarrassed too. As we walked back to "our corner" I kept thinking how the woman, the sleepwalker feels each time she has to help her grandfather go to the bathroom. I never wanted to look unhappy as she did. I admired her strength and courage for being there for her needy grandfather.

I still remember the smell penetrating and surrounding us, the smell produced by human waste, as if it is still here. Interestingly going to bathroom never smelled like that, not before not after, as if even the smell of urine and stool was reformed, radicalized and became extreme, like the rest of our pains and sufferings.

For many years, I had a hard time sleeping at night remembering things that had happened in this dirty place as if I were watching a horror movie with the best soundtrack, the best graphics, high definition, and in 3D... It occurred the day soldiers allowed us to bathe in the nearby Bosna River. The bad smell was not such a bad thing at all, and bathing in water filled with blood and dead bodies wasn't such a bad experience either. As a matter of fact, the effect on the smell's chosen participants in this new study was far more positive than anticipated. This form of liquid which resulted from the lack of proper hygiene, lack of water, soap and deodorants became our savior, as if the odor-water became more concentrated not only in intensity, but also in the quantity. The smelly-liquid substance produced by the human body seemed to have had a mission. The small salty drops with strong odor planned to bring some sort of liberation to us, to make us feel that there were still human instincts, needs and rights inside of us.

As we got into the Bosna River to refresh ourselves and wash up, we were watched by the Croat soldiers holding guns in their hands and making sure that no one tries to run away, or pull some act of defiance. Afraid that we might get shot, quiet and horrified of saying anything and speaking to anybody, feeling cheated of the right to bathe privately, and most importantly, being afraid to take off our clothes and thus attract one of them and become the immediate or the next rape victim.

In other parts of country, in other concentration camps run by both Croats and Serbs, there were many instances in which some had tried to escape and swim to the other side, some that had drowned themselves to end their nightmares, some that when sent to bathe were attacked and raped over and over and massacred in large groups. There were also those that were told that whoever swims the fastest will get a chance at freedom, but were shot as soon as they reached the other shore. There were also those that were seduced and made believe that if they give themselves without fighting they would be spared, a tunnel of possibilities would be lit. Some were injected by deadly drugs and then taken advantage of.

My Mom Sabira, my sister, Grandma Fatima, Grandma Zineta, my mom's sister Najla, and her daughter Ajla, Aunt Sheila, Aunt Amina, my mother's brother's wife Irma and her two children, my cousins and other relatives, neighbors and strangers, quietly tried to wash our bodies with soap. We couldn't talk. They ordered us to stay silent. We didn't take off our clothes all at once. I wanted to disappear that day. I wished to be invisible. My body had just stated to change, and I was ashamed of taking my clothes in front of anyone. I was trembling. My heart was beating like a baby's heart... thump-thump-thump-thump-thump-thump...

It was my mom who undressed us and washed us just like she did when we were babies. I was so embarrassed, and I couldn't wait to be done with it. Secretly, I remember thinking how the water felt so refreshing, so calming, even though it had a strong smell to it. There were some females in their bras and their old-grandma-type panties, but perhaps due to our friend smell, they weren't touched. The older men, and the boys, were waiting in line to be "washed" next. We weren't touched there, at that moment...

Nobody enjoyed this "bathing experience." Everyone was afraid to look up at soldiers--everyone except me. At one time, I slowly, raised my head and perhaps due to my puffy curly bangs, they didn't see me stare. All men, seven or eight of them cynically laughed, talked and pointed at the better looking women and girls.

One of them noticed that I was secretly spying on them and got mad. I remember thinking; *they can't do anything to me. I am just a kid. I didn't do anything wrong. I was just curious. That is not a reason to hurt someone?* But deep inside, I was frightened from that soldier's angry gaze.

81

I don't recall his face, but I remember his high arched eyebrows. He had two lines in between his eyebrows. Suddenly, we were interrupted by a scream from the crowd in this scary October scene – a bloated corpse in a leather jacket was floating just meters from us in the river. The poor man's face was eaten by birds, his eyes were taken out, a big part of his face was completely gone ... the bones on his face were showing; the cries, the screams, the fear of women and children, the smell, the bugs lined on the corpse's face are still very vivid in my eyes. Interestingly, this smell even frightened away our "Savior Smell."

It seemed as if even these two types of odors belonged to different groups, had different beliefs and values. As I turned my head to see the corpse, little girls, sick-old grandmothers and young moms screamed loudly, *"Mama, mama, what is that? What happened to that man's face?*

Both of my grandmas were out of our sight we couldn't see them. *What kind of smell is that?! Someone please get us out of here?!! I am scared mom, please hold me tightly!! Dear God get us out of here?!* The cries kept adding.

The soldiers standing nearby looked cynically as they laughed loudly saying, *"Heheheh... Hey you, k....e (b.....s) you should be afraid of us, not the dead man! Hehehehe... Dead man can't harm you! We can! Especially now, that you cleaned up! Hehehehehe!"* They kept going with the foul language and terrorizations.

Instead of acting right away, they let us watch, scream and plead. Perhaps they knew about the dead corpse in the first place? Perhaps they allowed us to wash up, just so they can enjoy the show? After about twenty minutes of begging and crying the terror ended — but the trauma of that day kept coming back years and even decades later. We were taken back, and given some sugar and water. That night, I couldn't close my eyes, not even for a second. The picture of the dead man wouldn't go away. Lamija fell asleep.

The following night, I slept an hour and then woke from nightmare sweats. My pants were wet, and my entire body was sweaty. I couldn't stop sobbing, trembling and shaking for a long time.

In my sleep, I saw everything. The man's name was Hamza. He was thirty years old. He had two kids; a boy and a girl. The boy was five-years old, and the girl wasn't even one. His wife had long black hair, reaching her lower back. She was beautiful, like a movie star.

As they were sitting at the dinner table, chatting and laughing, a group of Serbs broke in. They were drunken, and mad. They started to curse. The man got up, and invited them to the dinner table.

The six of them started laughing mockingly making ethnic jokes. The wife and the kids sat silently not uttering any words. She held them tightly, and tried to shush them. She covered her face, and looked down, trying not to get noticed.

Suddenly, the baby started crying. As she got up, she walked toward the room, to feed the baby girl. One of the Serbs, pushed her, and the baby fell down on the floor...

The husband got up to pick up the baby, but the other two, held him down. They tied his hands. They put scotch tape on his mouth, and put a gun to his five-year old son. Both baby girl and the five-year-old boy screamed. That is when one of them angrily yelled, *"Put the tape over the kid's mouths!!I can't listen to their cries any longer!!Shut them up, before, I take my knife and slice their throats!"*

The poor man tried to move. He couldn't bear

83

to listen to this. He wanted to stand up for his family. He wanted to save them, but his hands were tied. The young wife begged, as she knelt down on her knees crying and kissing the commander's feet.

She sobbed, and asked for their mercy, *"Please, don't' hurt us!!Please don't hurt my babies. They are innocent. Please don't kill them! Kill me, but let them live!"* she begged.

"We won't kill you. If we kill you, you won't suffer. We will be more creative, and we will make you watch! Before we do that, we will take turns, and" – the fat-bearded one said. *"Stop it!! Someone might hear, and come to their rescue!"* another Serb added. The infant moved her body. Her face got red and purple ... that is when I woke up screaming loudly, waking up everyone nearby.

CHAPTER 11:
Bosnia
June 1993

As we jumped up, someone turned on a flashlight, then passed it to our neighbor who pointed the flashlight at us. My mom was screaming and calling for her mother, who got transferred into our hangar a day ago. Aunt Najla and her daughter Ajla were in another hangar with Aunt Najla's mother-in law. Grandma Zineta was in her sixties. She was in poor health. Granny Zineta was heavy, and she just like the rest of my mom's side of family loved eating meat. When she walked, she walked slowly, bouncing from her right side to her left kind of like a penguin.

When mom screamed, she came within a second. She had her gray hair in a perm. She was a big woman, not so tall, but slightly taller than Grandfather Asim. She dressed nicely and stylishly and she wore make up. Her gray hair was always styled, and she wore lots of gold. It wasn't cheap gold, or one of those thin rings, bracelets, necklaces, earrings, or pearls. All her jewelry was expensive and thick. Grandfather Asim worked hard, so he was able to buy her expensive jewelry and expensive modern clothes.

My Grandfather Asim was a year younger than grandmother. He was slightly darker and shorter than grandma. She was the one who would get easily frustrated and angered. He was always, calm and cool. His only weakness was that once in a while he used spend half of his monthly earnings in a bar on his friends, food, good-looking singers and musicians – drinking beer and having good times –but he never forgot his family. He was so generous. He gave and helped everyone, even those that didn't deserve the help. He never neglected, and his family and he always gave them everything.

Out of all of his children, my mother had his heart. She resembled him the most. Her body movements, her gestures, her voice, the way she held her cigarettes and things she said, where identical to Grandpa's. She even looked like him the most. Mom Sabira even inherited Grandfather Asim's skinny legs.

Unlike Grandma who used to scold us for breaking stuff and getting into trouble, he never raised his voice. I remember him most by his big-heartedness. I loved him. I loved him not because he always gave us money – big bills, not small bills.

I loved Granddaddy Asim because of the way he was. He was funny and loving. Grandfather Asim used to have us sit on his lap and feed us with his hand, wipe our face with his napkin, and wash our hands with water. His black, mustache, and his smile will always stay with me.

Grandfather survived the concentration camp. He survived the starvation. His and Grandmother's house was burned, shelled, and they lost everything. They lived as refugees for years after the war in one room in the Old Court House in the City of Maglaj. There they had no private bathrooms or bathtubs.

Before the war, they lived in a huge bi-level house. They had land, farms, domestic animals, money and status; the war took it all. To feel "better", Grandfather started smoking cigarettes a half pack a day and eventually— two packs a day.

He died from Thromboangitiis Obliterans disease, also known as Buerger's disease. The disease is associated with tobacco use, and in extreme case it leads to amputation of legs and hands. His legs, toes ankles shins, thighs and his flesh were extremely inflamed, clotted, infected which led to amputation.

He died with a cigarette in his mouth.

Aunt Najla and my mom looked alike. Aunt Najla and Uncle Hadis had a gorgeous blond little girl name Ajla. Ajla was always energetic, carefree and fearless. She used to climb up the couch and jump. She inherited a lot of aunt's traits, but she looked more like my uncle. Her green round eyes and her long eyelashes stood out. She was extremely bright, outspoken and did well in school.

Ajla was interested in anything and everything. She loved to sing and dance. She had many talents. One time, she was even on local television dancing and singing in a competition. Aunt Najla gave Ajla everything. She had the best shoes, the most stylish clothes, and she was one of the most popular girls in her school. Ajla took private lessons in dance, singing, drama, English, ballet and she was very outspoken.

Tetka (Aunt) Najla was just a little shorter than mom. Unlike mom who was a housewife, Aunt always worked. She finished high school and kept going. She obtained additional training and received a diploma to work as a secretary.

My mom had dreams too, but she wasn't as lucky as my aunt. Mom had dreamt of becoming a nurse. She studied hard and received good grades, but after she finished eighth grade, my grandfather Asim stopped her.

According to the stories I heard, he was afraid that she would get married, and he would have nobody to help him with his land and farm. Mom used to have a long black hair reaching her back and she was gorgeous.

Back then a lot of beautiful girls went away to the city to study and got married. Aunt Najla was three years younger than mom, and by the time she completed her elementary education she was given permission to study.

Aunt Najla was a woman who "took care of herself." Her hair was always done. She used to have long nails, always painted in a different color, and she dressed nicely. She knew how to talk to people and loved to help others. She was tremendously ambitious. Anything she wanted, she got.

She used to stay with us in Zepce before she married. I used to hate to see her leave the house and go on dates with Uncle Hadis. I used to say, *"She was my aunt, and I didn't want to share her with anyone!"*

After some time, I learned to accept that she wasn't just mine, so I learned to accept Uncle Hadis as well. He used to bring me candy, chocolate and other treats. Many times, he invited me to go with them. They would buy me ice cream, new dresses, hair pins. As we would walk down the street, I would hold both of their hands and tell them stories. Little by little I became very fond of him.

The concentration camp shocked both Grandfather Asim and Grandmother Zineta. Grandpa took me into his arms, and Grandma hugged my mother. He ran his fingers through my curls and whispered into my ears, *"Amna, darling! It was all a bad dream! Relax. I need you to breathe in deeply."* He said calmly as he showed me how relax.

After sever trials, I managed to calm down a little. We hugged each other for at least five minutes, until mom panicked screaming, Lah-mee-yaah! *where are youu? Where is my baby? Help!"* mom whimpered as she fell onto the hard floor.

"Sabira! Sabira! My child! Wake up! Open your eyes!" – Grandma Zineta cried as she washed my mother's face with water. *"Ma-ma-aaa, ma-am-aaa,*

please, ma-mm-my-yy, open your eyes! I beg you! "

I wept. Grandpa Asim was taken out by some older men to get some fresh air, as he was losing his consciousness too. They had to hold his both hands tightly as they put a cold towel on his forehead.

This day had more trauma than I could take. The dead man at the lake — the nightmare — my sister gone — my mom dying — my grandparents... I didn't know what to do.

I hugged my mom as hard as I could. I kissed her whole face over and over, as I whispered into her ears, *"We need you! Open your eyes mommy! We love you! Everything will be ok!"*

Grandma Zineta was on her knees crying without stop. As I kissed my mother's hands, Grandma Fatima, and my father's sister Amina and walked in holding Lamija's hand. My mother opened her eyes, not knowing that sister was safe –

"Mama! Mama! You are alive! Dear God thank you!" I said as I kissed my mother and ran to my sister's arms. *"Lamijaa! You are alive too! Let me look at you! Turn around! Let me count your hair, to see if anything is missing! You have no bruises! Thank you God!"*

I was blissful that she was alive, but I had it enough for that day. I needed to get my emotions out, so I screamed at her, *"Shame on you! You selfish spoiled brat! How could you disappear without telling us?! How could you do this to us?! Don't you know that you almost killed mom? If mom would have died, I would have killed myself too! I swear! I would have! Then, you would have to live with the guilt feeling responsible for both of our deaths!"* I wanted to keep going.

"You are not my mother to boss me around and tell me what is right and what is wrong! You

have no right to yell at me! Stop acting so smart! Stop pretending like you know everything? Don't think you are perfect!"

We both sobbed as she yelled back while everyone surprisingly listened and did nothing. The guards weren't nearby. If they were, who knows what would have happened. She made me so angry; we had a difficult day already, and sis as always had to make things harder. I had it enough of her. I wanted to push her, and I know she would have pushed me back, but we were separated. Mom was in shock. Aunt Sheila took me outside the hangar with her, and Aunt Amina took Lamija somewhere with her.

That night I slept at Grandmother Meira's Aunt Sheila's and Aunt Amina's hangar. Lamija stayed with mom. What had happened was – Lamija woke up in the middle of night and she went to the neighboring hangar to visit Grandma Fatima and Aunts Amina and Sheila. Sister's childish curiosity, and her desire to end her boredom, caused a lot of stress that night.

One day, we heard a rumor that there was a "way out." Of course there was an "if" and "but" "what if?" "What was the catch?" and numbers of unanswered questions, worries and possible unwanted scenarios.

The rumor became more than just a gossip. We were told that those that wanted to "get out" and to be "freed" could apply to the Exchange Program. Those were approved to be exchanged would be released from the concentration camp.

The Exchange Program was an agreement that was arranged and to be followed by opposing sides, Croats and Muslims, Serbs and Muslims, and in some other places in the country Serbs and Croats. What this meant was, we were going to be exchanged and sent to a territory controlled by Muslims, and Croats would bring their people to Zepce.

Their relatives, friends, children, wives, dads mothers, uncles, aunts and cousins who lived or for some reason ended up in Zenica were going to be reunited with their loved ones. We, on the other hand, would go into the "unknown" not to be reunited with our family members but to...

Soon that day arrived. Aunt Amina, dad's oldest sister was transferred to work in the concentration camp kitchen. As a launch lady, every now and then, when the soldiers turned their heads for a second to blow their nose, when they knelt down to tie their shoes, when they went to use the restroom or got distracted, Aunt Amina in addition to being a launch lady worked as a "mailwoman."

Back in that gated place there is no hope, no life, and no love. Everywhere you look, all you see is darkness – the sky that used to be blue during day and full of stars at night was gone. The round circular yellow bright energy producing sphere was transformed into darkness too. The entire universe appeared as if it had been displaced, hit by a meteorite, or a large object. The only "bliss" in this place of obscurity that one could get was a letter from a loved one saying that they are alive.

My Tetka Amina, whose husband suffered a severe stroke just before the war gave us a letter that my dad sent us. The letter said:

Dear Sabira, Amna and Lamija,

I want you to know that I love you more than the entire planet. All three of you mean the world to me. I love you more than life itself, please remember that. I dream of the four of us laughing, running, playing and joking, just like we have done before. I dream of taking you far away from this chaos, and giving you all you could wish for. I dream of hugging you and holding you tightly, and never letting you go.

Even though we aren't together, I think of you every second. You are with me in my thoughts, in my heart. I believe that the day we are reunited again will come; however we must stay strong. We must not give up hope. We must believe and hope for better. We must not give up.

They can take our home, our cars, furniture and our freedom. They can't and must not take away from us our beliefs, our hope, our love and our desire to love, live, to dream and to be happy, no matter what might happen. I need you to promise me that, if we don't see each other again, that you will keep believing in good, believing in God, believing in yourselves and dreams, and loving and living life for me. I need you to know that life goes on, and that darkness doesn't last forever. This chaos won't last forever either.

I will always love you, no matter what. I need you to take care of each other and to stay on the right path. After a lot of thinking, I have realized that you have more chances of making it alive in Vranduk, than here. Add your names to the Exchange List, and get out of this place.

Go to Vranduk, to Berina's and Ahmed's house. Vranduk is still in our hands and you should be safe there. If you stay here, I might lose you, but if you go, there are some chances that you will make it. It hurts me that I can't protect you. This isn't a goodbye. We will see each other once again. I believe this, and you must too.

Yours truly,
Adem

CHAPTER 12:
Bosnia 1993

Aunt Amina was the oldest child of seven. My grandfather Adil, who died four years before I was born, passed away from a throat cancer. He died at a young age. He didn't get to live to fifty. Grandpa Adil smoked a lot. God bless his soul, he drank too. He was a strict father and a husband, but he loved his family more than anything. My dad, among four of his sisters and one brother, grew up in a poor family, a humble but reputable family. All the kids were brought up to be truthful, accountable, courteous beings. They were not afraid, not ashamed to take low-paying jobs. They believed that everyone that is healthy and capable should and had to contribute to the family's well-being. My grandma, Nana Fatima was a stay-at-home mom, who even though had no education, was a smart-woman and a brilliant mother and a wife.

According to some of the stories and memories shared by my dad, my aunts and my uncle Grandpa Adil did not own land. My grandfather's salary wasn't enough to feed a family of nine, so my grandma used to go help neighbors take care of their lands in return for fresh vegetables, fruits and even money. In addition to giving birth to eight children, that is including a son Onur who died as an infant, Nana Fatima was a super-woman. She cooked, she cleaned and she made clothes for her children. She took them to school. She washed their diapers and their clothes by hand. She also attended and bowed to my grandfather, who sometimes was too harsh towards everyone. He didn't know how to share and show love in any other way. It seemed as if his way of showing love was through strong discipline. He, like many other fathers at that time, was admired and loved by his children, not because he bought them new shoes, new clothes or any other materialistic objects, but because he taught them how to become considerate, respectful and respected people, those that had morals, those that valued life, and those that were beholden for anything and everything. Grandpa Adil wasn't a rich man. He didn't leave his kids money, land or cows; he left them something far more valuable, something that no money can buy, and that is poise, gratitude, consideration, perseverance and values money can't buy.

Aunt Amina had three children; two stepsons from Uncle Enes' s previous marriage and one biological daughter named Samia. Uncle Enes was a reputable photographer. He was eminent and esteemed before the stroke. He was married to a woman who died at the age of twenty four. She left him widowed with two little needy boys. The older boy was three years old, and the younger one was eighteen months. Uncle was twenty nine when he lost his wife. He was tall and very handsome. Hurt, confused, and terrified fretful he told his two small boys that their mother was still at the hospital. He hoped to buy some time and strength, and find the precise words to communicate to his two little kids that their mother is gone forever.

Uncle Enes was from Maglaj, a neighboring city. Since he worked as a photographer, he came on a business trip to Zepce to take photos from the famous *August Vasher*-Carnival – that is when he took a slight glimpse of Aunt Amina in the crowd. He didn't get to talk to her. He didn't even get her name.

He knew nothing about this girl — who she was? — Where she lived? — was she married? — did

94

she have children? All he knew about this black haired, blue-eyed girl of a medium height, and slim weight is that she looked like her and that if he ever had to get married to someone and fall in love again, it would be with this girl.

How could he find her? Where would he start? He tried looking for her at the Vasher but she was gone. After the Vasher, he asked around the city, and one of the neighbors directed him to Grandmother's and Grandfather's house. As he walked in, he couldn't keep his eyes off of her. She looked so much like her, it was unbelievable. He excused himself. He kissed my grandparents' hands and was told to sit down.

Uncle Enes talked to my grandparents and told them the reason why he came. He told them his whole story. They listened and they pitied him. After he was done, they said that it was up to aunt to decide.

Aunt Amina was so touched by Uncle Enes's heart-rending life story, that she broke her engagement right away. Three days later they were married. Aunt Amina couldn't replace the boys' real mother. She resembled her a lot, and this was a big plus. More importantly, she loved, took care of them and raised them like they were her own. They loved her and admired her and called her mom.

The war in Maglaj started in the fall of 1992. Uncle Enes joined the armed forces to defend our people. While holding a gun on the front line a mixture of anxiety, the panic, the nerves, the heart, the oxygen going to his brain, his hands shaking, his heart beating too fast, and his body sweating led first to a panic attack — anxiety attack — nervous breakdown — severe stroke — and finally, paralysis.

Baaaahm. He fell onto the floor.

After that they came to Zepce, as refugees. They stayed with us, and when we went to the concentration camp they went with us. Aunt Amina drove him in a agricultural and a garden dolly since they didn't have a wheelchair.

My father's sisters Amina, Asya, Berina and Leila were known as women that looked feminine and beautiful, but also as women that were physically as strong as men. They always worked hard to satisfy everyone, but they never complained.

Aunt Amina survived the war. Her husband survived too. He recuperated, and became almost his "old-self." Their house wasn't burned down, so after the war they returned home.

For years after the war, Uncle Enes walked miles on his two canes. His desire to live and his perseverance were outstanding. He went from being paralyzed, incapable of uttering words to walking miles every day, singing, talking, and even reprimanding Aunt occasionally.

CHAPTER 13:
Bosnia
June 1993

Tetka Asya is the second child Grandmother Fatima gave birth to. Asya was tall, slim, and light-skinned with curly light brown hair. Her dainty blue eyes were exotic sapphire that it made it hard for you not to stare at them when she talked.

She loved school, and she was one of the best in her class. After elementary school, she wanted to study to become a teacher. Grandfather Adil refused to give her consent, since the school was located in Zenica. She would have to travel every day. It was expensive, and on top of that, it would be "difficult to control young beautiful girls."

Family's reputation and name meant a lot at that time. Fathers were over-protective. They lacked proper education themselves due to the World War II. Most of them didn't understand the significance of education. Aunt Asya's dream of becoming a Math teacher was never accomplished. She did become an expert and esteemed worker at *Mahnyacha*, manufacture where she took extra courses and earned a great position and excellent salary.

Aunt Asya and Uncle Muhamed were friends for a year. Their friendship turned into a three-year long relationship, and a twenty-one years long marriage. They were perfect for each other. I never heard them argue or disagree. We used to go to their house on the weekends for get-togethers. Our parents sat down, they ate, they drank, they sang, they danced and enjoyed themselves. I remember Aunt Asya and Uncle Muhamed as one of the happiest and the most entertaining couples.

I love Aunt Asya because she was so easy to talk

to. I could sit and talk to her for hours. She was a great listener and a friend. With her everything was unpretentious, pure, and humble — there was nothing unnatural, nothing fake — no pretending.

My Uncle Onur was my father's only brother. He was Grandfather Adil's and Grandmother Fatima's fourth child. His house was located next to our house. I remember Uncle in his work uniform, all oily, with his hands full of grease. He was a hard-working man. He loved to joke with us, tease us, run after us and pretend like he couldn't catch us. Like all of my father's siblings, his eyes were blue too. Unlike dad, Uncle Onur had dark hair, and a slightly bigger, pointier nose. He was handsome. Slim, but muscular. He was good-hearted, generous, and caring man. Out of all of my uncles, I spent most time with him and Aunt Sheila.

Aunt Sheila was the calmest person I knew. She never got upset. She never got nervous. She was always positive, and nothing ever annoyed her or bothered her. Uncle Onur was the opposite. He wanted everything to be perfect. He was a perfectionist.

Aunt Sheila and Uncle Onur made a great couple. They complimented each other very well. He was the "fire" and she was the "water." It was a perfect mixture. They loved each other, and they showed their love publicly. Unlike my parents, who rarely kissed in front of us, and even when they did it was on their cheeks, Uncle Onur and Aunt Sheila kissed each other on their lips –regardless if the kids were watching. I didn't mind. I liked it. It was kind of romantic. I liked seeing adults holding hands and showing affection.

I secretly imagined having my prince charming hold my hands one day too. Aunt Onur and Aunt

Sheila behaved just like two teenagers. They tickled each other, they, watched funny, horror movies, they listened to loud music, and they loved life. They lived every day like it was their last.

After Uncle Onur, another child was born. His name was just like my father's, Adem. Adam died as a baby. Not long after, the second Adem was born. Dad resembled both Granny Fatima and Granddaddy Adil. As a child he showed extreme intellectual intelligence and creativity. He was very active in school and he was always one of the top three in his school in all sports. His wanted to become a Physical Education Teacher. Instead, dad became a carpenter. Once again, it was lack of money that led him to another direction.

When I was about five, daddy fell off of the roof. He got hurt badly, but nothing was broken. Three years before the war started in Zepce, he cut off his right thumb, his index finger and his middle finger partially. I was six when it happened. I was outside playing with my sister and my friends. Dad came home from his regular work. He ate, had coffee, and went to his basement workshop to make some extra money. Mom was a stay-home mom. She took care of us. She helped us with school work, she cooked, she cleaned, and she helped my dad in his little but cozy and enchanted cabinet Maker's Shop. There dad made windows, doors, cabinets, tables, chairs, shell, storages, china closets, dining room tables — anything and everything that could be made from wood. Dad was very talented and noble at his job. People knew him and came to him from all over Bosnia.

I came home to grab something to eat, and get a drink — that is when I noticed a group of neighbors standing in front of our house. Some were whispering — others were crying. From our basement I heard mother scream, *"Ah-deh-m"* I tried sneaking into our basement to see what happened, but I was stopped.

"Where do you think you are going young lady?" One of the neighbors asked.

"I want my mammy and daddy! I demand to see them! Now! Let me in! You are not a boss of me!" I impolitely shouted at our neighbor as I pushed her.

I was a problem child; that's what they tell me. I disobeyed everyone. I was right, and everyone else was wrong. Adults didn't know what was right for me. I was big enough to make my own decisions. I wanted to be tough.

I didn't like those "pretty girls" who stood in one corner who didn't want their shoes or dresses to get dirty. I hated them. That is why I liked hanging out with boys more than girls. They were cool. They didn't cry for everything, and they didn't go to their mom's for every little reason. I was bad all the way till I started first grade.

Seven, was a magical number for me. A year after dad's unfortunate accident we visited the neighbor that I pushed. Her words were, *"Sabira, what have you done with your old daughter? I don't see her in this room. She is gone. This girl, sitting on my couch is someone else. She is well-behaved, well-mannered, kind, and considerate. I hear that she is top in her class! I also hear that she wants to be a writer and a teacher when she grows up!"* I was so proud of myself. I realized how boundless it felt to be applauded. It made me want to advance myself and try even further.

Before, not many people liked me. After I changed my conduct, and became well-mannered, kind, and courteous people started liking me. I was pleased of myself, but mom and dad were prouder.

My Tetka Berina was born after dad. Unlike

dad, and Aunt Asya, Aunt Berina was extremely bright, but didn't pay attention in class. She loved make up. Aunt Berina dressed elegantly, modernly, and always found time to care of her looks.

We all loved Aunt Berina. She never yelled at us or scolded us for anything. She always stood up for us. She sheltered us from our moms when they would yell at us for misbehaving or causing trouble. I loved spending summers at her house in Vranduk. She used to play games with us, braid our hair, style it, cut it, curl it and blow dry it. Sometimes, she even did our make-up, our manicures and pedicures. She was always full of positive energy, and life. She rarely got upset or angry over anything. Aunt Berina, like Aunt Sheila was extremely patient, understanding and easy going.

Tetka Berina was into many things. She knew how to do anything and everything. She loved trade, commerce, business, buying selling, and making a profit. She knew how to design and make clothing. She knew how to bake delicious pastries, breads, cakes, rolls and much more. She could do anything. She believed in herself, and did everything with love – these were her secrets. In addition to being a mother, a wife, and being into sales, she was also the one you would go to for haircut, the one who would style, cut, color, perm and highlight hair. She didn't know how to sit and relax. She was great with people and everyone loved her. She knew how to make people feel good about themselves, how to be confident. She was great at listening and giving advice.

Her husband, Uncle Ahmed was also a good-hearted man. He was friendly, and loved playing with us kids. He used to let us play with his hair, pretending to be our client at a hair salon. He reminded me of Uncle Onur. He would get easily impatient and annoyed by injustice, and Tetka Berina would be the one to cheer him up.

Uncle Ahmed had black curly hair, thick black eyebrows, brown eyes and dark skin. Sometimes he wore black beard and black mustache. He was of an average height and weight. He had a mole on his face, and this made his facial features stand out. He too, rarely yelled at us, and he let us explore, jump, run and have fun, even if we made a mess.

Before the war, on my summer vacations, every morning he would get up, and prepare a rich, delicious breakfast that included my favorites. In addition to eggs, toast, cheese, milk, yogurt, jam, sour cream, sausage, and pancakes, there was always chocolate milk and Nutella. He made us feel welcome, and treated us like the most-respected guests.

When the war started, Uncle Ahmed chose to be the man to defend his family, not with a gun--but by staying to feed and provide for his wife, his son, his daughter and all of us – even if that meant hiding and avoiding to go to the front line. He knew that our mothers needed an adult male to take care of them (and us). He knew that if he would have gone like many other men to the front line, that there was a great chance that twenty-one of us would die from starvation. He defended us by being there for us, by finding ways to feed us. He walked days during snow, over the mountains, down the hills to find means to fill our empty stomachs. He was our savior. The others wanted to be our protectors; they tried to, but...

My Aunt Berina and Uncle Ahmed lived in Vranduk, one of the villages inhabited mostly by Muslims. Vranduk was a historical town. They called it "the old city." The first time Vranduk was mentioned occurred in the 1410. Vranduk was a place occupied and inhabited by different rulers, kings from

Balkans, Ottoman Empire and Austria.

It is unknown where the name Vranduk comes from. There are two of theories; one is derived from a verb *Braniti* to defend, and the other one if derived from a verb *Vrata* door. On the top of the hill, the large, stone castle stood. I remember my dad, my mom, Janna and me driving to Vranduk in our red Fiat. I remember staying in Vranduk during summer vacations for a week and sometimes two, and playing with my cousins Adna and Adnan.

Adna was two years younger than me. Even though we loved each other dearly, there were times when we didn't get along. Yes, there were times when we knew how to play nicely, but there were also times when we had to be separated physically from each other. Most of the time it was because of "she said this," "she said that," "that is mine," "don't touch it" or other incidents of that nature.

Adna had beautiful long light brown hair with natural golden highlights, big-blue eyes that looked even more glamorous in the sun. She was tremendously clever. She loved mathematics. I hated numerical problems.

I was kind of cute myself, but my lashes were not long as Adna's. People said I had beautiful curly hair, but Adna's hair was much longer and prettier than mine. She was one of those girls that always had beautiful dresses on. She didn't like to get in mud and dirty her clothes, but I did.

I was known as a tomboy. I played with boys. I fought with them. I wanted to be tough and I acted in that way, but deep inside I hid my softness. My mission was to seek trouble and to get in trouble. I was daily scolded for getting dirty, for ripping my pants, for staining my dresses, my blouses, and for dirtying and ripping my new shoes. My mom had to change my outfits at least seven times a day.

Both Adna and I were stubborn, and both of us loved to be in charge. We both loved to be in the center of attention, and that is, perhaps, why we pulled each other's hairs why we spit and cursed at each other and five minutes later would hug and play nicely as if nothing had happened.

Adnan was a year younger than Lamija. He and I never had issues. He did his things and I did mine. He never said anything to me, and I never said anything to him before the war. Later there were some situations when I would feel some anger towards him for eating too fast and not chewing his food in order to get more, when we would have to share a meal for two people with twenty two mouths.

I guess anger wasn't the only thing I felt towards Adnan. There were times when I felt jealousy because he would get an extra spoon of beans, or a second piece of bread only because he was skilled at eating fast. This was only an issue in the beginning of our starvation, but later, I would, like other kids, gained speed and eat without chewing, so that in the end each one of us would get a fair deal.

CHAPTER 14:
Bosnia
June 1993

Two hours after we received a message from my father to go to Vranduk, my mother added our names to the Exchange Program List, even though she knew that she might never again see my dad and our other relatives again. She also knew that there were chances that we wouldn't make it, that one of us, or all three of us could be wounded, raped or even killed. Staying in the concentration camp could also get us raped, wounded, killed, starved or even infected by a deadly disease. Mom chose the other alternative – the one where, even though we could also be dishonored, beaten or executed, it wouldn't be in that dreadful place. It would be outside the gates, outside the darkness. Very soon, we were told that we were approved to leave.

Just before we were exchanged, we were given a chance to go to our house and get some clothes and things we needed. Of course this meant being escorted by a Croatian soldier, and taking as little as possible. Sadly, my mom wasn't allowed to take me and my sister to see our home one more time before we said goodbye to Zepce. She went to pack up some stuff, followed and watched by a man holding a gun and pretending to be the Almighty, just like the Satan did in *Paradise Lost*.

It was time to apart. I stood static not taking my big round green eyes off of persons dear to me—

Grandfather Asim, Grandmother Zineta, Grandmother Fatima, Aunt Amina, Uncle Enes, Aunt Sheila, Aunt Irma, Samia, Amir, and other friends, and neighbors. Everyone was devastated. Grandpa Asim hugged us over and over. He cried like a child.

It was heart-breaking to see a grown man cry like that; I couldn't stop crying either.

Grandma Fatima was shattered— always in tears, blowing her nose and removing her glasses to wipe away her moans. I loved Grandma Zineta, but I was closer to Nana Fatima.

We shared the same yard. Our homes were next to each other. I saw her every day of my childhood. She wouldn't give me lots of money like Nana Zineta did. She didn't have lots of it. Every now and then, she would make delicious cookies; give us candy, chocolate and a treats. Every winter she would make us warm wool socks, sweaters, hats, and scarves.

Nana Fatima was one of those women who wanted to know all. After she would finish all her chores she would sit on her old-wooden couch and look out from her window. She had hard time hearing, but she always heard things you didn't want her to hear. She spoke loudly because her hearing was poor. When you talked to her you had to repeat yourself. She was the funniest old lady I have ever known — that is why all of us admired her. She used some old words that were out of use, so she always humored us. Nana Fatima had trouble pronouncing some words, and we always imitated her — antenna would be atenna fridge was a fidge and so on. She was religious, but once in a while a bad word would slip out of her mouth.

The funniest thing about Nana Fatima was the fact that she could sleep like a bear. Everywhere she went she would fall asleep. All she would do would be — put her head on her knees — then she would start Zzzzzzzzzzzz! — five minutes later she would be up. Sometimes she would wake up disoriented questioning *"Where am I? What time is it? How long did I sleep?"* – But most of the time she would get up refreshed as if she slept an hour. She was strong and courageous – that day when mom, sister and I were leaving the place of darkness – Nana wasn't herself.

Aunt Amina, tried to sustain herself too, but she couldn't. Uncle Enes observed from a dolly. He looked exasperated, and blue. My Uncle Nail's wife Irma and their two boys were there as well. They came from Maglaj to Zepce, hoping there would be no war in Zepce.

Uncle Nail was my mother's oldest brother. He was taken to the concentration camp too. Before war they were well-off. They worked for themselves, and they had a huge house. They drove expensive cars, they bought expensive clothing, jewelry and they went to interesting vacations. They always brought us great presents, and on both Eids gave us big bills.

Aunt Irma was a red-head, and she had freckles. She was pretty. She had long beautiful hair, and nice body. Uncle Nail had dark curly hair and he wore a pony tail. He was average height, and he had few extra pounds.

Uncle Smail was Grandma Zineta's and Grandpa Asim's second child. He was married to Senada and they had a son and a daughter. Unlike Uncle Nail, he stayed in Maglaj with his family. He too worked for himself and did well. He and Aunt Senada also had a big house that Grandfather Asim bought them. They had a business truck and made great money.

Uncle Smail had a unique smile. His white teeth were perfectly ordered and when he smiled his dimples showed. He was beautiful--muscular, and strong. His children had brand name clothes, and most stylish shoes dresses, outfits and accessories. Aunt Senada dressed elegantly as well.

My mom was the third child. As a child she was playful and easy to take care of. Grandma Zineta tells how one night she found mom hanging outside a window holding onto the window on the second level of their house. She was "asleep" – as a child mom used to sleep-walk. She was weak, and her immune system wasn't strong and she used to get sick often. She was very thin when she was younger, but as a teenager she started gaining weight and was never very thin again. Aunt Najla was the youngest child of four.

I couldn't keep my round big green eyes, and my long curly eyelashes off of people close to my heart – Grandpa Asim, Nana Zineta, Nana Fatima, Aunt Najla, Tetka Amina, Aunt Sheila, Uncle Enes in a dolly—like a baby I a stroller, except for he was a grown man, Aunt Irma, Samia, Amir, Amel, Ajla and other friends and neighbors.

Would I ever see them again? What will happen to each one of us? I didn't even get to tell them or show them how much they meant to me. If something was to happen to any of them, I will never forgive myself? I wish I had some power to undo the war. I wish things would be the same as before? Why is this happening? What will happen to us? I don't want my family to die. I don't want to die either. I don't want anyone to be killed, hurt or raped.

My Aunt Sheila stayed strong. She cried — there were tears in her eyes, but she controlled herself. She kept quiet for a long time — then she reasoned, *"Listen up! Let's not make this harder than it already is. We are terrified. We are distressed. We are losing our rationality and our faith! Our children need us! We must gather forte and bravery! We must not be fearful of this darkness that has fallen upon us! We must stay sturdy and enduring. Now, give each other hugs and kisses and walk away."* Aunt Sheila finished looking down as she wiped off a tear that disobeyed her. We kissed, we hugged and we left.

As we were walking toward the gates through the place of darkness, I decided to look one more time at this horrifying gated, gun-surrounded place filled with fear, innocent lives, hunger, smell, heartbroken, weak and powerless mothers, children and seniors. Walking toward the bridge I only saw ruins, torn down buildings, burned homes, bloody streets... We were told to go across the bridge that connects Preko, a part of the city that used to be inhabited by Muslims, our people. Preko was now an abandoned place. Almost all of the civilians, mainly women and children, were either killed or were lucky to escape to the safe territory. My aunts Asya and Leila with their sons got out.

Both Aunt Asya and Leila, cousins Adan, Harun and Yasin were in Vranduk now. They left on June 30th, 1993, the day we lost control of Zepce — the day we had to surrender and go to the concentration camp and the day her oldest son Kamil was wounded.

On June 30[th,] Tetka Asya survived a shock. She had a nervous-break-down. She was completely out of her mind. After she heard that her son was wounded, she ran out of her house while Croats were shooting and throwing bombs and grenade at Preko. She ran down the street walking over wounded soldiers, dead children holding soccer balls, murdered women on the ground with buckets of milk spilled, cats, dogs... As she ran, she screamed, she sobbed, she called his name. She carried his shoe, and each time she found someone in a camouflaged army uniform, she picked up their head to see if it was Kamil —

"Kamil! Sine (Son)! Where are you? Kamil! Please! Your mama needs you! Please don't leave me! I am coming for you!"

They found him alive, and he was taken to Zenica. Tetka Asya, Tetka Leila, Uncle Besim, Adan, Harun and Yasin left Preko. Uncle Besim helped carry Yasin and hold Aunt Asya. She was medicated, and completely distraught and heart-broken. It was too dangerous to try to escape during the day, so they waited for the night. Once it got dark, they left. They walked up and down Previla to Zeleca — then Begov Han. Next day, they walked to Vranduk.

This was going to be our route as well. The distance from Zepce to Begov Han is about six miles. Six miles isn't too much for an athlete. It is a lot for someone who is carrying baggage—someone who is being bombarded, shelled, someone who is holding two little girls' hands up and down a steep hill, and someone — extremely hungry, thirsty, needy of a shower, a comfortable bed — someone panicky and disturbed.

The only living humans left in Preko were the Muslim men trying to defend the land where their fathers were born, where they grew up, got married and brought children and grandchildren into.

As we were heading toward the bridge, we were lost in thoughts; afraid of what is going to happen, filled with melancholy, disappointment, anger, gratitude, confusion and so many other feelings. My mom, sister, and I, together with one hundred more or less other women, children and seniors, felt that the burned city Zepce, bloody streets, and dead children, dead women and dead elderly had felt a huge sadness and had shared our pain.

In the midst of all this sadness, a bunch of emotions and darkness, there was something supernatural about the city Zepce. It seemed as if the dead were more alive than those that were living. It seemed that both God-created and man-made showed human-like attributes. Everything considered a part of nature or that was related to nature, anything made in close team-membership of God and man, grass, trees, flowers, river, ponds, water, clouds, sun, air, objects, buildings, roads, rivers, trees, houses amazingly felt our pain, cried and prayed for us, all of us, even those that were either only misguided and lost in hunger for power and greed, brainwashed, or were simply evil.

CHAPTER 15
Bosnia
July 1993

When we arrived to the middle of the bridge, our thoughts and our emotions were interrupted by a grenade and shells flying all over – killing some. As soon as we saw the shells flying, blood, as soon as we heard that loud noise of the explosion, as soon as we heard cries and listened to some last prayers and pleas for help, our legs, our feet gained strength and speed. Soon we reached the end of the bridge.

Our hearts were racing, ready to explode under the pressure. We also instantly became instant Olympic class runners during the bombing. It was impossible to count the number of the lost competitors, those that didn't complete the run, not only because it was too many of them, but because those of us that were fighting for the medal and the recognition were so focused on winning and getting the gold for ourselves.

Once we reached our target, instead of feeling happiness, sense of accomplishment and pride for making it in this race, I turned around with sadness. The bridge was a sick red color, like after an accident where a truck spilled a load of highly concentrated tomato sauce, ketchup and red wine, escaping down the holes waiting to be united in a marriage with the Bosna River.

After we crossed the bridge we ran behind the nearest home whose only remains were two concrete walls. There we saw Uncle Muhamed, Aunt Asya's husband.

Uncle Muhamed always had a smile on his face. He was willing to help everyone at all times. He never knew how to say *"no,"* "I can't," 'I don't have time," or

"I am busy." He was a father who loved and cared for his three sons; Kamil, Adan and Harun. Uncle Muhamed was the first one on the list of volunteers to come and help out. He used to paint our house. All you had to do is say *"I'm planning to"*...and before you even had a chance to ask *"Could you please?"* he would ask *"What time and where?"*

He was of an average height, he had two dimples on his cheeks and he always smiled. When he spoke, he spoke fast. He moved, as if he was always in a rush. Uncle Muhamed and Aunt Asya's youngest son Harun was only a year younger than me.

Aunt Asya said that after mom had me, Tetka craved a girl – she had two boys, and she wanted to go for a girl — and Harun was born. Just before the Chaos began in Bosnia and Herzegovina, Harun, was hit by an ambulance. As a result, he started startling. My Aunt Asya said that his startling was almost gone, but as soon as the war began – it returned.

Uncle and Aunt Asya had two other sons, Adan and Kamil. Adan was the middle child. He was twelve when the war started. A lot of people would say that teenage years are the most difficult ones, when one is going through a lot of changes already, and when a father is something that each teenager needs, especially a son.

Adan like many other boys and girls lost his dad at a difficult age. Like many others, he didn't realize what it meant immediately. It didn't hit him hard right away. The extremities of loss, the emptiness, the broken heart, the void, the pain appears each and every time they see someone their age play soccer with their dad. The ache of not having a father happens each time they hear a song, watch a movie that involves the word father. The pain becomes something that one lives with until death, and even beyond.

A lot of children whose fathers and mothers were shot, slaughtered, burned or beaten to death live in denial. They live in the hope that their loved one's would just show up at the door, that they will be miraculously raised from dead. There are also those that ended up taking their own lives — those that overdosed — poisoned — jumped — hung — shot — cut their veins — take dangerous illegal drugs daily to survive with pain and — those who committed suicide, and contemplate suicide because they couldn't and cannot handle the damage. There were many who lost their reason, and ended up in mental institutions — many became addicted to anti-depressives and anti-anxiety pills — many whose lives and futures where taken the moment they lost their parents...

There are many children trapped in bodies of present thirty-year-olds, forty-year old, fifty-year olds and so on who are still going through the darkness.

Many, infants, preschoolers, elementary school kids, middle and high school kids witnessed with their shiny recipients of light, filled with mixture drops when their parents got shot — that saw their parents step on a mine — that saw their parents get butchered and cut in pieces — those that saw their mothers being raped and bleed to death — those that saw their fathers hanged, urinated on, spit on and burned — and there were many little girls and boys harmed together with their mothers and fathers simply for being Muslims.

Uncle Muhamed and Aunt Asya's oldest son Kamil was nineteen. Instead of partying with his friends, looking for girls and enjoying his youth, he had no choice but to take a gun and defend his mom and brothers, and ultimately put his own life in danger. These days people grow up at a later age,

Kamil was forced to become a real man at the age of nineteen.

On our way towards Kiselyak , Uncle Muhamed told us a shocking news that caused my mom to almost faint. *"Sabira, my Kamil was—"*There was a long moment of silence, moment of shock, moment of fear and hope. Uncle didn't get to tell us the rest, because my mom was in tears. After we calmed my mom, he went on.

"Sabira, listen, he is ok, they didn't... He was only wounded, so there are chances that he might make it. Kamil was wounded in his arm and in his buttock. No vital organs were touched, which means that he might make it. It all happened on June 30th, the day you guys were forced to go to the concentration camp. He will survive I know. He has to. He is too young to be taken. I'm not going to let them take him away from us!!!" my uncle said in tears. *"Dear God, thank you, thank you, thank you!!!! Please, let him get better, let him get a second chance....Ooh God, but he is only a child!" "How is Asya? Does she know?"* My mom kept insisting to find out the rest of the story.

"Well, emergency sirens rang the night of June 23rd, 1993. The next six days we tried to defend ourselves while you women and children, the sick and elderly hid in the basements. On the sixth day the Serbs arrived to help out Croats. They came with eight tanks. The night of the fall, Kamil and Miki were on the front line too. The next morning, June 24th, 1993 we came home because the Croats "signed" a "peace agreement" promising that all the fighting will stop. In it they gave a word that there will be no more war, and they will leave us, their neighbors, their classmates and their best men alone. As soon as all of our men returned home, half an hour after the

115

"agreement" the Croats started shooting, bombarding from all the sides including our territory. They had tricked us to believe that there will be no war at least not in Zepce, so that they can gain more control. Kamil fought all six days, and the day we lost control of the city he was wounded. Kamil was shot in his arm, and received 10 shells to his right buttock, but thank God he survived. He is in the hospital in Zenica, recuperating, and I know he will be OK." (It took three months for Kamil's arm to get better and to go back to defend us. Sadly this wasn't the only time he faced death. The second time he was shot happened on May 23rd, 1995, when he received a shell in his neck which almost killed him.)

Uncle Muhamed showed us the way to a five-hundred-fifty meter tall *Previla,* also known as *Orlovik*, a steep hill that surrounds Zepce. This would be our route toward the safer territory. He took us between the houses and places that were not so open to avoid being shot and reached by any of the objects of death. Our initial route was going to be *Preko, Hrastusa, Previla, Zeleca, Golubina and Begov Han.*

CHAPTER 16:
Bosnia
July 1993

As we walked towards Kiselyak, my mother and my Uncle Muhamed told us not to pay attention to the rotting corpses of cows, dogs, cats and other domestic animals. It was tough not to look at those unfortunate kitties, puppies, cows and horses. Some cows were shot in more than one place. There were dogs missing legs, kitties shot in their eyes and backs, black and white horses bleeding all over.

The street was filled with human and domestic animal blood mixed together. It was challenging to find a clean spot to step on.

There were holes in the cement made from grenades. The air was filled with the smell of explosives — the odor of animosity.

"*Mama, Tetak (Uncle) why are the cows, horses doggies, kitties and chicken bleeding? Why are they all over the streets? Who would want to hurt them and why? Do cows, dogs cats and chicken believe in Allah? Were they also hurt because they like us are Muslims? Why do people think that Muslims are bad and they should be killed?*" I questioned.

"*Honey, don't overwhelm yourself with too many questions,*" my mom had tried to shush her. That is when I added, "*But why, mom? Why are we being punished? I thought God only punishes bad people? I thought that if you don't lie, don't steal, don't hurt others, if your heart is not rotten, if you are honest, respectful, loving, compassionate, good things will happen to you. Why are bad things happening to us?*"

"*Amna, God will punish bad people. Their*

time will come. You must continue believing in God. You have to love Him, and live with the principles that daddy and I taught you. We are not being punished. This isn't a punishment. This is only a test that we must pass. God is testing us to see if we will continue to believe, love and live our lives in faith and goodness." Mama explained.

My sequence of questions and my desire to find out answers and to understand what my eyes of a nine-year-old, and my little vehicle of contemplation, and reasoning were interrupted by a loud noise of some kind of explosion. *Booooooom!!!!! Baaaaaaam!* We went down on the ground, as mom shielded us with her body.

From that moment on, we kept walking silently, at a higher speed. I don't recall any other conversation between mom and uncle. Soon we reached Kiselyak; one of God's gifts to human kind, this fresh, cold, life-saving and thirst-quenching mineral water source.

I remember coming to Kiselyak to get mineral water with Samia, Aunt Amina's daughter. Samia was a tall, slender young woman, with honey-colored eyes and beautiful facial features. She had stepped into womanhood, and was at an age of dating. Samia was a year younger than my cousin Kamil, she was eighteen. I always looked up to her. I wanted to be that pretty one day. I couldn't wait to be older, so that I could have a boyfriend who brings me flowers, candy, chocolate and takes me out to dance.

Being pretty during a war is not much of a blessing. It is not a gift, it isn't a form of pride, it isn't a tunnel with intersections of choices and opportunities, nor is it a road to recognition and fame. On the contrary, being pretty and showing it to the world meant a road toward destruction, toward loss,

118

life of endless suffering and pain, countless nights of nightmare, insomnia, tears and even death.

Unlike today, during the age of Facebook, Twitter, MySpace when everyone posts beautiful pictures, and feeds off the compliments, exposing oneself and showing their beauty openly, letting everyone see it, comment on it and put a "Like" mark, during the war one only risked being attacked, eaten away, and stolen by the predator.

Being beautiful meant that one could have more chances of being robbed of her virtuousness, her pureness by the drunken, misguided armed forces. As a result, many mothers dressed their daughters in baggy clothes; they had tried to hide their gorgeous daughters so that they are less beleaguered by the hungry, irrational men.

Sometimes it had worked, other times it hadn't.

There were also those mothers that dressed up their girls as boys, those that cut off their hair so that they could appear boyish-looking. There were also those moms that were forced to watch their daughters getting raped — those who were tied to a chair with their mouths tapped shut so that they couldn't scream.

Others were allowed to scream for help that would never arrive and there were mothers that begged to be violated in order to spare maidenhoods of their children.

All of these innocent young girls were marked and scarred forever.

There were also girls that took their own lives after they were numerously raped by not only one of these men, but countless. There were also those girls that got impregnated — those that had babies — those that took care of them, and loved them in spite of everything that happened.

That is what Selma did in the novel <u>Remember Me</u>, by Sanela Ramic Jurich. The very first time Selma held her baby, she said; "I realize I couldn't let him go. I would rather die a horrible death than part with him. This small, innocent creature was a part of me. I felt a strong need to protect him from the world."

Selected number of these mothers stayed silent about it. Countless others blamed themselves for being violated. While some tried to find peace by sharing their stories; hoping to stop genocides, killings, rapes, discrimination and injustice.

It is true that some of these slaughterers, rapists had been brought to justice in the Hague Tribunal international Justice System located in Netherlands where war criminals are to be persecuted and punished) — but there are also many monsters that are walking freely — many of the war criminals made profits — lots of them left the country — other monsters changed their identities and are living freely among us.

CHAPTER 17:
Bosnia
July 1993

Uncle Enes, Aunt Amina, Samia and one of her brothers lived in Maglaj, a city where my mom grew up. Aunt Amina's other stepson worked and lived in Serbia. My Grandfather Asim, and my Nana Zineta, my mom's parents were also people with strong values and belief in hard work. Unlike the father's family, my mother's family owned some land, cows, sheep, and chicken. They didn't have to wait to be called to work on other peoples' properties. In addition to having their own crops, fruits, vegetables, milk, cheese, sour cream, eggs and other dairy products for the family, my Nana also sold some of the dairy products and fruits and vegetables as well. My Grandpa Asim was also a blacksmith. He made shovels, axes, horseshoes and lots of other things that he sold at flea markets all over Bosnia. His black smith's shop was located in Stari Grad, the Old City in the city of Maglaj, where my mother, my uncles Nail and Smail as well as my Aunt Najla grew up.

My mom used to tell us stories of her childhood. When she was a child, and even a young lady, the kids would watch the cows and goats eat that green grass decorated in pink, red, purple, yellow and orange flowers of all kinds.

According to my mom, whenever she thinks of her childhood, the first sense and feeling that takes her and flies her back into the days of innocence and curiosity, is the smell of grass, trees and flowers which she describes as the smell one feels when they enters a flower shop filled with colorful plants grown without any chemicals, or additives used to grow flowers now a days. Those plants at that time resembled the smell of the very first lilies, orchids, violets, dandelions, roses and many other God-given forms of nature that make one fall in love on the first sight, the first smell, the first touch.

My favorite part in listening to my mom talk about her past was the part in which she described the relationship between a man and a horse, the excitement, the adrenalin and the understanding one would have with this amazing creature.

I never rode a horse. I never saw my mother ride one either. I imagined both of us riding it together; up the awesome hills and mountains, getting to the top of them and looking down at the cities, valleys, villages, rivers, ponds, lakes, houses, farms impregnated with potatoes, carrots, cabbage, cucumbers, greens, onions, green beans, black beans, pinto beans, corn, garlic, strawberries, cherries, grapes, apple trees, all these gifts given first to Adam and Eve and then all their children, grandchildren, great-grandchildren, and their children, and us to enjoy and indulge in, not only to fill our bellies but also to taste, smell, chew slowly on, observe and feed our brains, our souls, our eyes, our noses...

As the oldest daughter, my mother had to take on a lot of responsibilities. While grandfather was in his blacksmith's shop, grandma working at a farm or milking cows, and doing other chores, uncles were helping out grandpa or watching cows and horses up the hill. At a young age, mom learned to cook all meals. She washed everybody' clothes manually, she fed the chicken, and she took care of her younger sister. She had no time to play. Everything was timed. If something wasn't done the way it wasn't supposed to, Grandma made her start over. Nana was tough on mom, that's why she makes the best food in the world. Her older brothers were always demanding – *"Give me this! Pass me that!"* ordering her around while they sat on the couch and relaxed. She didn't mind. She loved them dearly.

When mom got old enough to start dating, every time she would go out with her friends, my uncles followed her. She wasn't allowed to wear make-up. If for some reason her friends lent her their lipstick, mascara or an eye shadow to use, and she ran into uncles — she was in big trouble. She used to carry napkins, and make up remover with her all the time.

I was a stubborn baby even in my mother's womb. I didn't want to get out. I gave her such a difficult time, that she was about to be sent into C-section to have me. Her water with me broke a day before she checked into the hospital. Back then, they had no pain medications at all. Mom said when they told her that she gave birth to a baby girl she couldn't stop crying. Mom cried because she knew that this little baby girl would have to go through the same pain one day too. It is like she knew — she felt it...

Mom had always been unperturbed. Things didn't bother her that much. She had abundant tolerance and great nerves. Unlike dad who would get irritated by injustice, societal imperfections, people who lied, cheated, stole, egoistic individuals, mom didn't stress out about it. They were the perfect opposites. They balanced each other very well. They completed each other's gifts and faults. Dad needed mom and she needed him. Together they were one. As much as they occasionally disliked each other's differences, they knew that this is what made their marriage and their love complete.

Dad fell in love with mom first time he met her. Her long straight black hair that reached her lower back, her big brown eyes enchanted him. She kept ignoring him, but he persisted.

Mom used to wear skirts up to her knees, corresponding jackets, and comparable boots. With just a lipstick, eyeliner and perfume, every time she walked down the street everyone looked. She wasn't thin, but she had everything a man wanted. She was beyond gorgeous. Her facial features were as if they were drawn by a famous artist. Mom had a great voice. She loved to sing, when nobody was around. Her voice sounded compelling, but she never worked on it. Lamija got mom's voice. I didn't — I got her patience.

CHAPTER 18:
Bosnia
July 1993

As we reached *Kiseljak,* my head was filled with imagination once again. As I closed my big green eyes I saw a white horse whose skin was white as snow and eyes as black as summer nights with two large magic wings. This horse wasn't an ordinary size. He was big enough to carry five people any place they would desire. Everything about him was magical. He had an ability to talk, listen understand and fulfill any wish you have.

"Horsy, Horsy, could you take us some place far away from here? Some place where we could be safe and happy, but before we go could you please make a stop and get daddy too? I want us to be a happy family again. This time all four of us could visit the sea. We could swim in its emerald waters, walk on its sidewalks made out of colorful stones, touch, smell palm trees, indulge in strawberry, chocolate, vanilla, banana ice cream, and sit in one of those restaurant patios drinking juice from those fancy glasses with little umbrellas and new flavors while watching people walk, talk and laugh. Later, we could visit the circus and watch all performers perform different acts, stunts, laugh, eat popcorn and drink coca cola. Dad could take pictures of us. In the evenings we could walk down the streets, once again enjoying ice cream. This time we could buy soft-serve swirl ice cream and talk about everything we've seen. As we walk, we could see young lovers holding hands, looking at each other and seeing no one and nothing, besides each other. Finally, before we go back to our hotel, we could ask someone to take a picture of all four of us.

Before I had a chance to hear the horse's response my mom interrupted. *"Girls where is the backpack with photo albums? Where is it , what have you done with it?"*

Lamija's cheeks turned red as red apples and her voice became shaky. In her honey colored eyes, two tears appeared. As she spoke the tears ran slowly down her cheeks towards the ground.

"Mama, I swear to God it wasn't my fault. When we were running across the bridge the backpack became too heavy, and in the fear I accidentally dropped it. " "Kcheri (daughter) it is all right, don't cry. It is not your fault that our pictures are gone. What is important is that we remember good days, and that we safely reach Vranduk. Pictures are only material things, and even though they have meanings they can be replaced with memories. Don't worry angel, we'll take new pictures after this nightmare ends. Don't cry."

My mother said with eyes full of tears as she hugged both of us and kept us close to her for what seemed to have been a long time. Tetak Muhamed watched, not articulating any words. After we calmed down we said goodbyes to him.

It was August thirteenth, nineteen-ninety three. According to some eye witnesses, *Tetak Muhamed* was walking with a bag of long-expired cans of food that were donated from the world. The planes used to drop packages and bags of food, soap and second-hand clothing that no one wanted to wear, expect for people like us. For us everything was great, since we had nothing. Everything that we owned was stolen from us, and we were happy with the old, too-big, too-short shirts, pants skirts, jackets and shoes.

Not everyone was lucky to get a piece of clothing, a bag of expired beans and a can of food. In the places, where planes passed through, and released the packages, people acted as little kids jumping in excitement, pushing each other just to catch something. They competed against each other and played roughly for the price. Watching, and participating in these moments was an indescribable experience. You had to be there to see it, to experience it, in order to understand the happiness felt when a package reached a hand.

Uncle Muhamed's role in the army was the one of a cook and a carrier. Before the war, he enjoyed preparing food, trying new recipes and cooking for everyone. Now, in addition to his chef role, he was also the grave digger. Every time a soldier was shot, Uncle dug the hole.

On August, thirteenth, he was carrying food for others, when one of the round metal objects filled with tuna, goulash or sandwich meat fell down on the ground. Knowing that food was limited, and that one can meant a lot, he kneeled down to the ground to pick it up. That is when the sniper shot him.

The were-man holding the sniper seemed to have been playing a game killing his time and amusing himself. He waited for Tetak Muhamed to pick up the can and then bummmmmmmmmh. As he fell down on the ground the blood flew in all directions. The food that day wasn't delivered on time. A father, a husband, a son, an uncle, a friend, and a neighbor –was gone. Aunt Asya stayed in bed for weeks. She never remarried.

CHAPTER 19:
Bosnia
July 1993

Mom took the bigger traveling luggage in her hand and I took the smaller one. We decided to give Lamija a bottle of water to carry, since the bag with our baby pictures and growing up photos was lost. The fear that we had before reaching *Previla* was different and perhaps smaller than the one we had as we climbed up this five-hundred-fifty meter tall hill.

This time, our fear doubled. Instead of being afraid of being shot or killed by a shell, a sniper or a land mine, we were also afraid of losing our physical strength and falling down the hill. Sweaty, with shortness of breath and unusual breathing rhythm, we reached the top of *Previla*. An acquaintance named Enis greeted us with a look that showed both happiness and pity at the same time.

"Sabira, how are you guys? Good to see you arrive here safely. How is Adem? Where is he? How is the rest of the family? Where is your sister Najla, how is she doing after the news?" he asked wanting to find out the answers to his questions quickly.

"Wh-wh-at d-d-o you mean Enis? Please tell me that Hadis is alive and that there is nothing to worry?!" My mom said in a stuttering voice. *"I'm sorry Sabira. I really am. I hate to be the one to tell you the bad news. Hadis is in a better place now. He is a shahid, (the one who is with God), and you shouldn't panic — your girls need you. They need you to be strong for them!"*

He was shot by a sniper. Tetak Hadis, was an educated man. He was an engineer with knowledge of four languages. He used to work in Alger for a while. As a little girl I used to admire him and wish to speak that many languages as well. I couldn't understand how a person could learn that many languages, and not to mix them up. He spoke English, French, German and our language. When I was little, I wanted to be just like him when I grow up. I wanted to travel the world and speak many languages.

It took a while for my mother to calm down. Before we left towards *Zelecha* which was located on the other side of Previla, Samia's boyfriend showed up. He volunteered to show us the way down the hill. Many nine-year olds would have shown jealousy or wished to have been smaller, because their six-year-old sister was occasionally carried down the five-hundred-fifty meter tall hill, but I didn't. If it wasn't for him who seemed to have been sent to us as a protector and a guide, I don't know if we would have made it down the hill. This, comparing to running across the bridge and being bombarded and walking up the hill, was so far the scariest. What frightened me the most was the fact that we had to walk as slow as possible, and use our feet — to break in order not to fall and roll down the hill — and hit a tree or a bush — and die just like it happened to some of them...

The tall trees stood above us and sheltered us from the explosives — they watching us with empathy. The sound of wind that shook the trees whispered to us that everything would be fine. Why in the world did they send us this way? Why couldn't we take the road, as normal people? This wasn't normal. Everything around us was abnormal. The forest the plants, the ground, the flowers appeared to had been the same forest, plants flowers and ground from *Hansel and Gretel*. As we walked down Previla there were things we shared with Hansel and Gretel. The Evil Witch wanted to eat us just like it happened in that story. The only difference between the Evil Witch and them was the fact that Hansel and Gretel were able to defend themselves and destroy the Witch. We would have to wait and see if the Evil would die.

Miki carried sis. I walked down the Previla carrying one rucksack on my back and another smaller luggage in my hands. My back hurt badly. My neck was stiff. My legs felt numb. The pain was excruciating. I wanted to scream loudly—instead I bit the inside of my lips and I ground my teeth as hard as I could.

After a stressful and frightening walk down the hill, we reached Zeleca. I threw the backpack and the luggage on the ground. I picked up my arms and I stretched them as much as I could. Since we had no more water left, we took a sip of the pond water coming down the mound. The brown water wasn't clean, but we didn't mind. First we washed our faces, refreshing ourselves. Then we cupped our hands and drank it. It felt so refreshing and rejuvenating, as if it was the purest water in the entire universe. We took a short break and we continued.

The majority of once beautiful homes, only those that belonged to Muslims, were torn down and destroyed. Some homes were completely demolished; the only remains of them were the foundations. Other houses were missing roofs, levels, windows, doors and were full of shells. In other towns, villages and cities, lots of houses and the remains of homes were scribbled with graffiti with derogative, degrading and threatening words; *"Die Balije," "No room for Turks on Balkans" " We will slaughter all of you"* and many more hurtful phrases and words.

Zeleca looked just like one of those deserted towns inhabited by souls invisible to the living lost and stuck in the world in between. Passing through this village was scary for one. There were no people.

For others, it was frightening to see so much destruction, all those vacant homes and remains of homes. Soon we reached Begov Han.

Unlike Zeleca, Golubina and Begov Han were packed with people and refugees. As we arrived to Begov Han we were greeted by men dressed in army outfits holding guns but smiling at us and welcoming us. One of the soldiers told us that the refugees were sheltered in an elementary school located nearby.

The idea of sleeping in a school was intriguing, since we knew that those that fell asleep during class would be awakened feeling pain in their ears, or being asked to show their palms to be "taught a lesson" with wooden sticks. Other teachers castigated daydreams by asking them to stand in the corner facing the wall, and turning their back toward the class doing nothing, and saying nothing for minutes or hours. I was never had to be punished. I loved learning. I listened and respected my teachers at all times.

As we walked into a classroom, there were no desks, no globes, no maps no students, no student work posted on the walls and a blackboard washed with no writings on it. This room was once a homeroom. Now it looked more like a gloomy place, with nothing in it except frightened, sad and lost mothers and children, sitting quietly in corners on boxes.

This classroom and all classrooms in the school were filled with refugees from different places. Next to one of the windows there was family of three; a mother, a son and a daughter. The mother seemed to have been young, but her face was red and swollen, as if she has been crying non-stop for days. The boy must have been a couple of years younger than me. He wasn't in school yet. The girl looked eleven. She was a little taller than me, and she started developing

131

into a young lady.

While we were eating dinner, the boy got up and started walking toward what seemed to have been a bathroom. His mother and his sister kept sitting quietly, not asking anything and minding their own business. As the boy stood up and as he started walking towards the door, I remembered my first day of school.

One of my classmates got up and started walking towards the door when the teacher approached him. *"Marko, where do you think you are going?"* she asked.

"What do you mean where am I going? I am going to pee!!! That is where I am going. " he answered.

At that moment the whole class started laughing loudly, some of us so loud that our bellies were cramping from the laugh. This boy, unlike his mother and sister whose minds seemed to be wandering, played with a blue truck and seemed to have been unaware of the situation his family was in.

The young girl kept shaking. Occasionally, she articulated some words that were tough to identify. There were moments when she moved her hands, as if she was pushing someone away. She couldn't bear to look at herself or anyone else. She couldn't eat. She couldn't sleep. She was so embarrassed, so miserable, and it seemed as if she refused to look in her mother's eyes.

Late at night when everyone slept, the girl kept covering her face and her breasts. Unlike the rest of us, she sat the entire night. Her eyes were opened. She stood leaning her body towards the wall. She strongly held a teddy bear, patted his back, and whispered to him.

After a long time, I managed to fall asleep. I

slept for a short time, and once again I woke up screaming and sobbing. In my dream, I saw the girl get raped. They tied her up. She kept begging to let her go. They laughed, and cursed. They spit on her. Then, they took a huge piece of wood, knocked her unconscious.

After ten of them took turns, she woke up. Then, they brought her mom, and forced her to watch her mom get violated too — there was so much blood on the hardwood floors. The mother and daughter were down on the floor. There were no more tears. No more words. The little boy played with is blue truck, as if nothing happened...that is when I woke up missing dad.

Where was he? What was he doing? Was he hungry? Was he cold? Was he in pain? Did they hurt him? — Stupid question — of course they did — those men were evil.

A wooden chair caught my eyes. I saw dad tied onto a wooden chair that he made for the soldier interrogating him and tormenting him — asking him to admit something that he didn't know — something that he did not do. Dad's head was high. He was mentally strong. Dad was brave, for every time the irritated Croat bruised and made father's body bleed with the other chair that dad made before the war — dad swallowed the pain.

The torture continued until the pesterer got tired and decided to give dad a break for that day... I blinked, and within a second I realized that dad was still in the place of the darkness. I walked to that chair and pushed as hard as I could; It fell onto the door. Everyone looked up. I wanted to take it and throw it out of the window.

CHAPTER 20:
Bosnia
July 1993

The second day, we were to walk another six miles. As we walked toward Kovanici, Topcic Polje, we kept taking breaks. Mom and I walked two meters in front of sis who kept asking; *"Are we there yet? Could we stop and take a rest? Could I have more water? When are we going to eat?"*

It was a hot and humid day, so the walk was tiring. We knew we had to hurry to reach Vranduk before the night arrived. Back in Zepce we were told that our neighbors Tina and her husband Kerim whose house was across the street from ours lived as refugees in Topchich Polje. We made a stop, ate little refreshed and kept going. Nemila was the next town. It was one town before Vranduk, which would be our home for next five years. There are two tunnels that you must pass through on your way from Nemila to Vranduk. The tunnels had no lights. This was the fastest route to Vranduk, and in order to get there you had to walk through darkness.

Once we got to Nemila, we sat down at a bus station to take a break. Lamija's skinny feet were bleeding. Her ankles were swollen, and she complained that her right ankle ached.

I was exhausted too. My back was killing me from the heavy backpack that I carried. Each time mom asked if I was okay, I lied. My back and shoulders felt numb, while my right hand was throbbing from pain. In addition to the backpack that I carried, I helped mom carry another traveling bag. She held one handle with her left hand and I held the other with my right.

A short fat blond man in his sixties stood in a

corner observing and listening to our conversation. *"Mama, I am hungry!"* sister complained.

"Here is an apple. Wait till we get to Aunt Berina's and Uncle Ahmed's house." Mom explained.

"Excuse me! I couldn't help but notice! Didn't one of you mention Berina and Ahmed from Vranduk?"

"Berina is my sister-in-law and Ahmed is her husband. We are from Zepce. We were in the concentration camp. My husband and other family members are still there," mom added. *"I am from Vranduk too. Berina and Ahmed are very nice people. Everyone respects them. Ahmed helped me last year on my farm. My wife goes to Berina to get her hair done. By the way, did you need a ride?"* the man offered. He was sent to us when we needed him the most.

We got into his old station wagon Passat and we left. As we drove, I remembered the day I got out of the hospital after I had a surgery. Back then dad drove the small red Fiat.

I was born with three tonsils. This unusual condition created some breathing difficulties. Doctors recommended that I have the third one removed. At the age of three, I had a surgery in Zenica. After the surgery I stayed in the hospital by myself to recuperate.

There was this boy who was very annoying. He used to bug me all the time. His name was Faruk, and he used to take my doll and pull her hair. I told the nurse about his behavior, but they did nothing, so I decided to take things into my own hands. I was tired of hospital. The food tasted bad. They had all these rules. The nurses weren't friendly.

I missed my mom and dad, and I decided that it was time for me to go home. I had no idea where home was, but I was determined to leave. I took my things, I packed my bag and in my pajama I sneaked out. I walked towards my right.

The exit was that way — at least that is what I thought. As I tiptoed trying not to make too much noise, I got caught. I ran as fast as I could. Five or six of nurses ran after me —they caught as I reached the exit and they took me back into the room. I screamed — I pleaded — I cried — nothing worked — they took out a sharp needle —minutes later I was sleep.

That is my first and my oldest memory. I was three years old. We drove through the tunnels – the same place where I narrated the story from the hospital to my parents as we drove back home from Zenica. The only difference now and then was the darkness. Then, the tunnels had light — now they were dark. Also, then dad was with us—and we were driving home—now...

As we got out of the tunnels there it was — Vranduk, place surrounded by beautiful hills, forests and roads, farms, stone and flowers. Bosna River ran through this village. During summers the water was green. After the rain it turned brownish yellow. During winter time it changed from green, to brown, to emerald.

On the top of a small hill, a fortress was built out of stones with small windows having views from all angles. The fortress itself was unordinary and magical. As kids, we dug holes using sticks, hoping to find a treasure like Huck Finn and his friends had done. The idea was initiated by me. I loved history, and one day after school I went home and took a nap. I dreamt of gold hidden in the castle, and I told my friends about it. The fortress was a place where we played Soccer, Dodge ball, Basketball, Tag You're It, and Hide and Seek. It was also a place where older kids hung out in the evenings, had their first kisses and dates in.

For me, fortress was a place where I would go to meditate, and pray. Here, I would day dream. This was a place of escape from starvation, nightmares, fear, ache and emptiness. Here I would bring my notebook and write poems journals and open up.

A week after we arrived to Vranduk, I wrote a letter to dad. We had no words from him. Mom wrote a letter as well. We took our letters to Zenica to the UNHCR. We sent a letter every week for nine months. He received none. In my first letter to dad I wrote:

Dear Dad,

I think of you every second. I miss you so much! I dream of us being together again. Mom, Lamija and I are doing ok. They miss you a lot too, and they are sending you kiss. We are safe. Please don't worry about us, because there is nothing to worry of.

Aunt Berina and Uncle Ahmed are very nice to us. They feed us; they clothe us and give us everything.

I am doing really well at school. My teacher, and most of my classmates are very nice, and they try to cheer me up. Literature is my favorite class. I love to read stories, and write about them. It makes me forget that you are far away.

Dad, please come to us soon. I dream of you all the time. Sometimes we are together, but other times I see you in pain. I see them hitting you, pushing you and making you work hard. I see

137

bruises all over your body. I see you bleed. You look very thin. Your hair is long, and you grew a beard. They give you very little food and water, and they make you sleep on cold floors, without mattresses or blankets.

Dad, I worry about you all the time. Please tell me that you are fine, and that they aren't hurting you. Please promise me that you will get out soon. Promise me that we will be happy again. I want you to know that we love you so much, and that you are in our hearts and minds every second. Take care of yourself!

Love,
Amna

Here in fortress of dukes and kings, when all the kids would leave, I would stay. There, in the citadel of the powerful Balkan, Turkish and Austrian rulers, everything I would see would take me to him. At one time, the fortress served as a prison, just like the place where father was. I would look at a stone from a fortress and picture my dad carrying large stones up and down the mountain, and working as a free laborer for Croats. He looked ill, and thin. I almost couldn't recognize him. His azure eyes were pushed in — his cheeks were flat — his hands were shaking. I couldn't understand how a thin man covered in skin and bones could carry such a huge stone.

Back in the place of darkness they interrogated dad — abused and then starved him like all other imprisoned men. Instead of having captive men sit in the concentration camp and do nothing, the Croats decided to put them to work, and use them as free laborers.

This was a time to make money, to get wealthy. Those that had nothing before the war had everything now. Now, they drove their neighbors' cars. They slept on their neighbors' comfortable beds. They sat on their neighbors' luxurious couches. They walked on their neighbors' costly rugs. Their wives wore expensive gold, diamonds, sapphires, pearls and other jewels and their children rode new bikes, and wore brand name outfits and shoes.

Back in the fortress there were also those days when I would call out his name, and talk to God to bring him back to us alive. I used to think that the castle was magical and that its echo could be heard far away. I imagined it had hidden cameras that captured and sent everything any place you wished it to be sent. I wanted dad to see me.

That is why the next five years of my life I spent most of my time in the fortress. Almost two decades later, I secretly believed that this castle, even though it was remodeled and turned into a historic attraction and a museum, that it belonged to me, and only me. For years I had the same dream over and over —flying — from top of the fortress through the green valley over the emerald Bosna.

After a long day of walking, we arrived to Vranduk. Here we were welcomed by my Aunts Berina, Asya, Leila and Uncle Ahmed. They embraced us and took us in. That night we went to sleep late. We stood up sharing our experiences and comforting each other.

CHAPTER 21:
Bosnia
October 2008

Aunt Leila was my dad's youngest sister. She had beautiful light green eyes and short, curled and highlighted hair. Her long and thick eyelashes were even longer when she wore mascara. She would wear red or pink lipstick, a little blush, and leggings in different colors. She always wore pointy-high-heels.

She was of an average height, but comparing to my father and his other sisters, she was the shortest one. Leila was a beautiful woman with one noticeable thing about her face, and that was her nose. As a little kid she and my Aunt Berina were playing, and as a result of their play, Aunt Leila broke her nose.

She ended up having surgery, so her nose was lowered because the bone from it had to be taken out. Even in this condition it was beautiful, and many people had no idea that it was ever broken.

Tetka Leila's birthday was only two days before mine. Her birthday was on my Anniversary. She always fought for justice and fairness. She spent a lot of time thinking and upsetting herself about the imperfections of this world and its people.

There were times when she was stubborn and hard-headed only because she thought that she was right. She loved helping others. Before the war she worked as a social worker, where she met and helped lots of people. She was a good person, and wanted everyone else to be good too.

There were times when she would act strong and tough, but deep inside she was soft and frightened. She hated hospitals and tried to avoid them as much as possible. Every time she would walk into a doctor's office or a clinic she would faint. I guess you could say she had nosocoemphobia. Not long after we arrived to Vranduk, about a month later Leila heard the news... News that affected her significantly. For ten months her monthly cycle was gone. She went through a serious stress that led to a nervous break-down, extreme anxiety and depression that she couldn't recover from.

There were many stories and accounts about the death of Uncle Besim. One of the stories is that he was wounded and taken to a concentration camp in Herzegovina. Another story said that he was transferred to Zagreb, Croatia. Someone said that he was found by a local imam and given a proper burial in a cemetery. Another witness claimed that they found him dead in a bathtub of one vacant house in Preko.

Nobody knows exactly, how and where he was killed, and that led to suspicion and denial of his death in Aunt Leila's mind. Years later, even though there appears to be a grave with the remains of his body inside, Aunt couldn't accept that he was gone. Uncle Besim was the best thing that happened to her.

He was the man of her dreams. He was handsome, tall, well-built and had great personality and sense of humor. Their marriage, unfortunately a short one, was one to die for, the one seen only in dreams, read about in books and seen in movies. His death left a wound in her heart and made a hole in her soul. This led towards the most painful and the longest death of all.

Her son Yasin was a small child, who was robbed of a normal childhood; a life without a father and a life with a mother hurting and suffering for years. First he lost his father, then, he became an orphan at the age of seventeen when he lost his mom too. Yasin was a very energetic boy. He loved to run and jump and joke. He was always full of energy. He had a contagious smile; when he smiled you smiled too.

As the years passed by, even after the war was finished, Aunt Leila kept it to herself. Instead of moving on, asking for help and accepting the realty, she failed to help herself and recuperate. It looked as if she swore not to love anyone ever again.

It appeared as if she gave up her hope, her desire, and her love for life. She became a prisoner of the cycle of negative energy. She lost herself in it, and couldn't find a way back. There was also something else unique about her. She was afraid of doctors and hospitals. The war and the loss made her lose trust in people.

Every year, she kept getting deeper and deeper into depression and anxiety. Years after the war, we were told that she would lock herself inside her apartment. She became afraid of going outside. She lost herself in the past.

The moment she heard the news about Uncle Besim's death, became the bullet that ripped her heart, and kept it bleeding for years. Tetka Leila started hearing things. She started seeing things. To ease her suffering she smoked cigarettes, one after another. She ate very little and she didn't take care of herself. She became very sick and she developed tuberculosis, and died in her early forties.

I called her to tell her that I was pregnant with Sara. She told me to eat a lot of bananas — she ate them with Yasin too. She was the only one who called every year from Bosnia to wish me a happy birthday.

Tetka Leila died, just after Yasin turned seventeen, as if she had patiently waited for him to become old enough to live alone. Aunt Leila stopped believing in herself. She stopped believing in love, and her life came to an end. She got lost in the labyrinth of the darkness and couldn't find a way out.

Her death was the most touching one of all, and the most tragic one as well. Unlike three of my uncle who were killed by a gun, and died shortly after, she was dying slowly and painfully for years.

The war was far more destructive and painful than one would think. Many human lives, both physical and emotional were taken during the chaos, but many of us have been wounded internally, and have been hurting for years.

Many of us who are physically alive seemed to have been transformed into being lost, weak, and confused. In other words, we are not people we were meant to be, and were supposed to be. Some of us have found ways to cope and then to accept and live our new lives.

Many have given up by taking drugs, stealing, fighting, overdrinking, overeating, not eating and accepting defeat. Unfortunately many orphans, victims of rape, abuse, survivors of concentration camps, mothers, fathers, aunts, uncles, grandparents, friends, neighbors and acquaintances had gone as far as taking their own lives, thus ending the suffering. Sadly, Yasin was left all alone in this world full of drugs, alcohol, lack of jobs, and a country filled with huge economic and political problems as well as poverty. Without a job, without a direction in life, what will happen to an orphan like him?

CHAPTER 22:
Bosnia
July 1993

About a week after we came to Vranduk the rest of our family from Zepce joined us. Aunt Sheila, Uncle Onur's wife, and their two sons Amir, Amel, Grandma Fatima, Aunt Amina and Uncle Enes were exchanged from the concentration camp as well. Aunt Berina's and Uncle Ahmed's two bedroom house was a shelter and a home to twenty two beings. Unlike us, whose exchange route was over Previla, they were allowed to walk using the roads.

Uncle Enes was handicapped, but he didn't have a wheelchair. Aunt Amina drove him in a dolly from Zepce to Vranduk. Since Grandma Fatima was in her seventies, she had a hard time walking. They drove her in a dolly too.

Their arrival meant less food, less space, and less room to sleep. We would sleep on floors of each room of the house squashed like sardines. Aunt Berina and Uncle Ahmed used to sleep in the entrance of the house, since all other places were taken by us. There were nights when Uncle Ahmed and cousin Kamil slept on a balcony.

Aunt and Uncle hadn't finished building their home, so there were no showers or bathtubs either. Even though the house wasn't big enough for all of us, we were happy to be alive and to be together.

I remember nights talking with my cousins, laughing and sharing stories. We were so grateful, so happy and loving towards each other. The one and only good thing about war was that it made us love each other more, respect each other more. The war brought us closer.

They say that the moment we all are equal and

we all have the same, the love becomes greater, but the moment this balance is broken, the greed, mistrust, pride and desire to be better, to brag awakens.

Aunt and Uncle had no land to farm. Before the war they had jobs. They lived in a village, but worked in the city. They weren't farmers like others. Sometimes, neighbors brought some leftovers, some wheat and corn flour, some milk and cheese. This wasn't enough. Uncle Ahmed, cousins Amir and Adan and Amel used to walk days to buy cigarettes.

Miserable, tense and irritated people smoked and made merchants wealthy — the oppressed found some liberation in smoking. Uncle Ahmed, cousins Amir, Adan and Amel walked on foot for smokes – during hot, humid days – and – during the extremely cold and snowy days and nights.

After they purchased cigarettes, Aunt Berina went to Zenica and sold them to make some money and buy food. With the money earned from cigarettes, Uncle Ahmed and Aunt Berina baked bread, rolls, cakes, sweets and cookies that were also taken to be sold. I remember the delicious, sweet smell of the pastries and the bread that they baked.

I used to close my eyes — open my mouth — lick my lips and imagine how everything tasted. Those sweets were not for us. We couldn't try them, we couldn't taste them. They were made only for those who were able to afford them.

After the cakes and cigarettes were sold, Tetka Berina bought flour, beans, potatoes, rice, oil, bread, salt, sugar, coffee and milk — enough to feed all of us for only two days — after that we were at the mercy of neighbors who had little food for themselves too.

People starved all over the country. The food was so expensive — those who had gold used to trade necklaces, bracelets and rings for flour. Everything we had — they took. We had nothing to trade. If anyone in the village needed any physical labor or any other help we were the first to go. Sometimes, they paid us in apples, potatoes, tomatoes, beans, milk or cheese. It didn't matter, as long as it was something.

Everyone had a job including the youngest. Some made food. Others washed the dishes, vacuumed, dusted, washed clothes using our hands, organized shoes, cut wood for the fire. One of my jobs was to help out with homework and school assignments. I didn't mind doing chores and keeping myself busy. It helped me keep my mind off of things.

One that did bother me was some kids avoiding their chores and being messy — Lamija and Adna used to do that. They enjoyed seeing me mad and they did it purposefully. They hated the fact that I was always the "perfect one" who did everything right. I know I wasn't perfect. I was far from perfect — I was mature. I took life seriously and I didn't want to make it harder on my mom and my aunts.

Aunt and Uncle tried to provide for us. No matter how much food they came up with, it never was enough. There were no shells, no sirens, no shooting in this town, but there was another type of aggression – starvation.

Since lack of food became an issue, Aunt Asya, Kamil, Adan and Harun found a vacant house in Begov Han and left. Grandma Fatima and Aunt Leila and her son Yasin left with them too. Aunt Amina and Uncle Enes found a shelter in Zenica. Aunt Sheila, Amir and Amel and three of us stayed at Uncle Ahmed and Aunt Berina's house. Even though everyone else was gone, and we had more space, the starvation became extremely severe.

There were days when we had nothing to eat —

146

nights when we went to bed without supper with our bellies aching. On some days we picked certain types of grass and ate small pieces of it.

On the outskirt of the village, there were rich trees of cherries, apples, peaches and pears. The owner lived on the other side of the town. Under different circumstances I would never do what we did only two times — we were left with two alternatives — to survive or — to become ill and die from malnutrition and starvation.

Besides, this was something that all kids from the neighborhood did, even those who had enough of food. The "forbidden fruit" that we picked after we jumped over the fence and climbed up the trees had the juiciest, the sweetest, and the tastiest sensation ever.

A week later, the owner moved into his weekend home on this plantation. He brought his two dogs with him and a shot gun. No one dared to go near that place again.

After we came from concentration camp we brought lice and scabies with us. Aunt and Uncle had no showers or tubs, since the house was still under construction. I was so self-conscious and I felt as if everyone avoided us in the beginning. Everyone in the village knew we had it. Even though nobody had ever said anything, I used to feel ashamed, embarrassed as if everyone pointed their fingers at us and laughed.

We were the first refugees that came to Vranduk. In 1995, a large group of survivors from Srebrenica and Zepa, located in Eastern Bosnia arrived – after the biggest genocide and massacre in Europe since the World War II occurred.

The starvation, lice, scabies and adjustment to all of this was forgotten for a day, when Uncle Onur,

147

my father's brother was released from the concentration camp. We were told that he became too sick to work in the concentration camp. Uncle Onur was imprisoned in *Shestica*— The Room Six — the place where the worst war crimes in Zepce occurred— where the harshest beatings, and the most difficult interrogations and tortures happened.

They questioned him over and over, they tried to manipulate him, they tried to have him confess something that he didn't do, and each time he refused they took turns hitting his head — his ribs — his lungs — his hands — his toes over and over with rifle butts. I pictured uncle Onur crying and begging them to stop.

They threatened him and told him, *"If for any reason you get out of this place alive, you must never tell anyone who and what we did to you or else your family will die! We promise you that"* Uncle Onur told Aunt Asya some things they did to him, but he never told anyone who did them. I've heard that daddy was in that place too.

Why they let him go — I don't know. He had nothing to confess. He was too thin and too ill for anything. He was harmless, and useless. Now that they couldn't use him as a laborer, he was an additional mouth to feed. A man too-sick to be beaten and abused, and a man they had no news or interest of keeping any longer, was released. Being forced to sleep on the floor, not fed properly, and forced to do hard labor on rain snow and ice Uncle Onur became very ill.

He was to come with a train at sharp noon. It was before noon. All of us got ready and left toward the train station to welcome Uncle Onur.

The happiness filled all of our hearts, especially the hearts of Aunt Sheila, Amir and Amel. Aunt

148

Sheila lost her mother at an early age. Her father remarried. Her mother's brother, her uncle and her aunt took her in and raised her as their own.

She was a tall, slim woman with wavy brown hair and brown eyes. She wore glasses. She was always calm. When she ate she ate slowly. She used to look at each spoon carefully before she put the food in her mouth. She chewed her food in slow motions. She walked slowly, she talked slowly, and she even worked slowly. There was no rush for her. I don't ever recall seeing her angry, raising her voice, or hitting Amir or Amel.

Uncle Onur was the opposite. The only time Amir and Amel would "get it" was from him. Amir had thick, bushy, but beautifully shaped black eyebrows. His hair was black and straight. Amel, on the other hand, looked as if they were not genetically related at all.

Amel had light brown eyebrows, light colored-eyes and long, blond curly hair. His hair made him look like a girl. Amir took after his mother. He was always very calm, cool and easy going. Amel was the one I argued with constantly. He was the one to push me, to anger me, annoy me, and made me cry, but regardless of it, we had a great loving relationship.

Amir was five years older than me. Amel was only three years older, so I spent more time playing with him. As we were getting older, our cat and dog relationship became more peaceful. Now my closest cousins were about to be touched by the sun. For them the darkness was to be gone. They were about to see their father after a long time.

For the three of them, this was the happiest day since the war started. I was joyful for them. There was also some sadness and envy inside of me too. Secretly in my heart I envied Amir and Amel. Their father was going to be with them once again, and mine was still in that place.

As the train stopped and as the travelers came out, a tall, skin-and bone man, with a beard, gray hair and weak body came out smiling. I noticed his once beautifully teeth were half gone. Aunt and cousins ran to him as fast as they could. I wanted to run too, but I decided to watch them first.

It was beautiful to see a family reunited again, hugging and kissing each other repeatedly. There were tears in many eyes including mine. Uncle Onur and Aunt Sheila kissed on their lips. We watched and cheered as we applauded them.

Uncle Omer brought us a letter from dad. This was the only confirmation that he was alive. The letter said:

Dear Sabira and my Princesses,

I hope that this letter will find you. I wrote many letters before, but I never received one back. Now that Onur is out, I am positive that you will get this letter. Please don't worry about me. I am fine. They are treating me nicely. I hope that you are well too. I miss you girls so much!! I hope that soon, they will let us out. When they do, I will run to you and hug you for days. I won't ever let them take you away from me! I won't let anyone ever hurt you. Please, stay patient. Our reunion will come soon. I love you so much!! I am sending you kisses and hugs, and I look forward seeing you soon!

Love
Adem

Uncle Onur and dad had a special relationship. Unlike most brothers who fought and disagreed on issues they got along most of the time. Mom and Aunt Sheila were even better. They never argued over who gets what and things of that nature. The same went with my aunts. They always looked out for each other and helped each other in every way. Back in that place of darkness, dad used to part his meals with uncle and bring him an apple, a loaf of bread, a magazine, an old crossword puzzle, every now and then after a long day of work.

Uncle Onur got out during the strongest starvation in the country. A couple of months after uncle got out, we were sitting down eating breakfast. I'll never forget that breakfast... Uncle Onur ate very little. Since the breakfast that day was small, instead of finishing off his portion, he divided it into two. He gave one piece to Amir and the other one to Amel.

I'll never forget Lamija's face and words; *"You guys are so lucky to have your dad next to you. You are so blessed to have him share his food with you,"* she said sighing. Uncle's cheeks got red, as he put his head down. He realized what happened, but it was too late. The damage was already made. There was no going back.

"Will I ever see my dad again? Will he ever share his food with us? Is he ever going to hold me? Kiss me? I wish my dad was here. If he was here I wouldn't have to go to bed hungry. I know he would find a way to feed us. If he was here, I wouldn't have to wear that old and ugly boy's jacket, or wear those tennis shoes three sizes bigger than mine!" sis said in tears. I got up and I ran outside.

I was so annoyed and exasperated—I was fed up with the war — starvation — life — everything. I ran as fast as I could and I climbed up the fortress walls. I was standing high, above the old city. I stood still. I closed my eyes. I raised my both right and left arms and evened them with my shoulders — the breeze felt refreshing — and the wind tickled my cheeks and made me giggle — I felt liberated as I was about to...

What is the point of living if there is so much pain?

*I wanted to end it all—once and forever—I wanted to feel nothing—I wanted to think nothing—I wanted to have no needs—no necessities—no emotions—I wanted to be free like a bird—I wanted to fly—I wanted to...*a leaf flew on my cheek and tickled my face.

I opened my eyes and I looked up in the sky — there it was — a happy face looking down at me — smiling at me — I just couldn't do it.

A few years later, Uncle Onur died. He never fully recuperated from the tuberculosis that he got in the concentration camp. Times were tough. The medicine was expensive, and healthy nutritious food was pricey too. He desired life and fought with his illness. He wanted to be there for his wife and kids, but he lost. His passing in his early forties just wasn't natural. His life was taken by "them, back there in the room six."

Times got harsher and harsher. We became thinner and thinner. We ate less and less till we got to the point where we had to go our separate ways. We started looking for other alternatives.

Someone told us that Zenica had many refugees from all over Bosnia. All public and government institutions were turned into shelters that provided food donated by the UNHCR. We knew that if we stayed in Vranduk hunger would kill us or we would take our own lives. As a result, we moved to Zenica.

There, we found a shelter in what once was a

daycare. We were "guaranteed two meals a day" a breakfast, and dinner." Only a year ago, this place was filled with kids running, jumping, playing, drawing, writing and reading. It was a happy place. It was a second home for many, and it was filled with positive energy and happiness. Now, this place was turned into a sad shelter full of refugees whose homes were burned, family members killed and imprisoned — many that survived torture — many that were raped and maltreated.

This place was crowded with refugees and the lines for food were huge. Sometimes we would have to wait hours to get our small portion of bread and half a cup of beans. Lots of times the food was late. There were also periods when after waiting two hours in line, we were told that there was no more food left — we were told to skip a meal or both.

A couple of times Maria, a Croatian lady invited us in and fed us. She lived in a building located in the alley of the daycare. She was one of few who stayed good. She didn't allow herself to be brainwashed and misled.

Her values and morals were so strong that they couldn't be easily broken. She lived alone. Her husband died long ago. They had no kids. Instead of eating alone, she invited us a couple of times and shared her meal.

Once she even lent us her shower to bathe. It was one of the nicest things anyone did for us.

For few months I would go to the market place and sell soap that we received to exchange it for food. A lot of refugees did the same.

We were given a choice. Our choice was to stay clean, or to stay hungry. Most of us decided that staying alive and not starving was the best choice. Back in the daycare, we had public showers.

Sometimes there was water. Other times, there wasn't.

On the occasions when we did have water, it was cold, almost unbearable to shower in. As far as electricity, most of the time, we had none. Candles and lamps helped us see at night. However, those were considered luxuries.

Some days my mother took us to her relative's homes where we bathed and ate, but most of the time we waited in lines at the Daycare place.

I recall the day when I lost consciousness and fainted because of hunger. *"Amna, wake up, wake up my life! Two of you mean everything to me!!! If it wasn't for you, I would—*

Please, please open your eyes! Please, please!!! Don't do this to me! You'll break my heart!!!If anything happens to you or your sister I'll take my own life. I won't be able to live without you!!!" mom kept repeating these words as she washed me with water.

A group of refugees circled looking sadly. There were refugees from Brcko, Maglaj, Gradacac, Bosanski Novi, Prjedor, Kozarac, Zepa, Srebrenik, Srebrenica, Maglaj, Doboj, Jajce, Sipovo, Mrkonjic Grad, Prnjavor, Foca, Vlasenica, Orasje, Odzak, Samac, Jablanica, Tuzla, Glamoc, Prnjavor, Trebinje, Kalesija, Cazin, Grude, Foca, Gornji Vakuf, and other cities and towns all over Bosnia and Herzegovina.

Soon I opened my eyes, and one of the refugees took out a cracker and gave it to me. After the panic ended and everyone left to their own little beds, we returned to our room filled with fifteen kids and five adults.

Here in Zenica I enrolled in school. School became my escape from hungry, crying babies and kids, smelly diapers, lice, scabies and chaos. The days when I attended school were the days I looked

154

forward to. School is what kept me going.

Late at night when I couldn't sleep, I transferred my feelings, my worries and my pain on pieces of paper and turned them into short poems that rhymed. Writing became my therapy, medicine for my soul and a way of staying sane.

Back in school my teacher was Serbian. His wife was Serbian too, but they stayed in Zenica. He was short and heavy. We loved him. When he spoke, everyone listened. He had a way of getting you to pay attention by doing nothing unordinary. Every now and then he made a joke.

There were kids who were born and raised in Zenica, but there were also those who were refugees from other places from Bosnia. We all got along, and we helped each other. The school wasn't every day, so all students were eager to come to school and get back to normality.

I met a girl from Kozarac. Her name was Zehra. She stayed at a school with her two aunts and her sister. Her both mother and her three-year old brother were shot in front of her eyes as they tried to run into the woods. Her mother was five months pregnant with another boy. Zehra's father and her uncles were taken into concentration camps, and she knew nothing of them.

She had black eyes and short dark blond hair. She was dark-skinned and she had one dimple when she smiled — and she did smile. She smiled to the point where she would start crying loudly and had to be taken outside. Each time I felt sad, I just thought of Zehra, and my troubles would go away. She moved moved to America shortly. I never forgot her.

Chapter 23:
Bosnia 1994

"Allaaaa-huuh-akbar-uuh-llaah-huuh-akbar..."
The beautiful voice from the *Minaret of the* Mosque echoed. I looked at time. It wasn't a time for a prayer. I realized that the house was empty, and that I was the only one still in bed.

I got up. I went outside. Aunt Asya and Kamil were there too. Grandmother Fatima was praying silently. Her eyes were puffy as If she cried. Mom was on the ground. She wasn't moving — Aunt Asya was washing mom's face with a wet cloth and calling her name. Mom looked pale. The voice coming from the minaret was announcing mother's death — she must have died — she lost sixty pounds in such a short time due to starvation and stress — she probably died to save us from starving.

"Mama! Mama! I am sorry! Please don't go! Please don't leave us! I promise I will eat less from now on. I will split my food with you from now on — just come back! We need you!" I cried over her body.

Lamija wasn't there. If she died, why was she breathing? Why was her chest moving? Something didn't make sense. I know someone died! I feel it! If mom is still breathing—that means that she is alive.

She opened her eyes and she sobbed.
"Amna, he is gone! Your daddy is gone! I am sorry baby! I am so sorry! You no longer have a dad! Now it is just three of us! We must stay stronger than ever! Daddy would want us to! Please Amna? Please promise me that you will be ok! Promise me that you won't let this get to you!" mom kept going.

This time I knew for sure that I wanted to die. I wanted to go with my dad. I wanted to be where he was. I ran toward the fortress—I already had a plan there was nothing and no one that could stop me from doing it... Cousin Amir ran after me. He held me tightly and we cried. *"Daddyyyyyyyyyyyyy! Daddyyyyyyyyyyyyy!!!!Daddyyyyyyyyyyyyyy!!!!!!*

I woke up shaking and crying, calling his name. The next day I went to school with bus. I was in fifth grade. I attended school in Nemila and that day we had no bus on our way back. There were two tunnels that connected Nemila and Vranduk. The first tunnel was shorter; the second one was longer. Both tunnels had no light, and we had no flash lights, lighters or candles with us either. We had our sticks that we touched the walls with to make sure that we walked on the sidewalks in case cars drove through the darkness and we weren't hit.

My friends Azra, Amra Ajna and I always walked together. That day I kept it to myself. I couldn't stop thinking about dad and the nightmare from the night before. We walked two miles on foot.

Ajna suggested that we test our strength and see who was the strongest of all. When it came my turn, I fought like a pro. I pushed Ajna onto the ground and I wrestled her — then I sat on her stomach. Amra and Azra looked at each other in disbelief. She was in pain. She was crying.

I lost myself — and I went too far. There was no way back. I took my backpack and I ran home. I hated myself —I wanted to vanish — I wished to be unseen — I wished to go back in time and undo the damage — it was too late. I don't know what happened that day.

I had a feeling that mom would find out what happened, so I told her my side of the story. As soon as I was done, Ajna's mom, furious and distraught, came and screamed loudly, *"Listen to me now! Shame on you and your family! You stink! You are dirty! You have nothing to wear! Your bodies are full of red spots and scabies! Your hair is full of lice! You lost your homes! You lost everything! Why? — I will tell you why? You are no good! If you were good, you would still be in your homes — but you were not! God is punishing you!"* she kept going.

Mom told me to go and play. That night a huge piece of glass from old china cabinet fell on my left leg as I tried to put some dishes away. There was blood all over. The clinic was in Nemila, and due to lack of transportation we didn't go. I still have a big scar on my upper thigh. Mom didn't even say a word to me about the fight. No timeout, to talks, nothing.

She and I didn't talk for a year. She approached me first. Her mom talked to me afterwards too. She never apologized, but we talked.

CHAPTER 24:
Bosnia
March 1994

The UNCHCR got involved and intervened. The barricades had to be removed. The concentration camps in Zepce had to be opened for the visitors and family members. Those wanting to go from Zenica to Zepce and vice versa were allowed. For us this became an opportunity to visit our dad. We knew that it was risky, but we took a chance.

Some of the Bosnian mothers and children from Zepce, those that weren't exchanged were imprisoned in their own homes. Mom's aunt, Aunt Aisha, a school teacher wrote to us. She told us that it was safe to visit, and if we wanted to we could stay with her. Her husband, Uncle Said was an accountant at the local school. He was made to kneel down, walk and "Oink" as a pig, as some of his former clients hit him, spit on him and laughed.

Without a lot of thinking, we left towards Zepce. We took the train from Zenica to Begov Han. We walked from Begov Han to Zepce. After we rested, changed and ate at Aunt Aisha's house, we went to the place where dad among others was still imprisoned. I don't remember where it was. I remember the large gates that surrounded it. There were soldiers that "greeted us smiling politely" and asking us who we came to see. I put some mascara on before we left Aunt Aisha's house. I wanted to be pretty for dad. I changed at least five times.

Her house had three levels – it was one of the most beautiful houses in the city. Everything was organized and neat. I sprayed myself with her perfume and I put some gel on my curls. I grew a lot in nine months. I was so nervous, so anxious I kept going up and down the stairs at least twenty times before we left.

What should I say to him? Should I hug him or kiss him first? I have so much to tell him—Where do I begin? What if I forget something? What if he only nods and pretends like he listens to my stories? I hope he will love me like before? I kept driving myself insane.

I wore an old outfit. It wasn't my size — we got it from one humanitarian organization. It was a little big, but it was clean. The lice and scabies were gone. My hair was shorter — it was easier to take care of it. The outfit wasn't my favorite, but it looked better than the rest of clothing that I had. It was a long green dress reaching my toes. I had a warm black coat on, and black rain boots that I wore all year around.

The guard told us to follow his younger college. The other one took us to an area that look like a place where the captured prisoners ate. There were tables and chairs. It looked empty and melancholic. We sat down and waited. Couple of table to our right a family kissed and sobbed. I wanted to get up, because my nerves couldn't keep still, but the soldier watching gave me a look. From far away there he walked — he was unrecognizable — a tall man — all skin and bones — with tears in his eyes — and a smile of joy. He was held by two soldiers holding rifles as he pulled them as fast as he could. Mom got up. Sister was up too. She and I were about to push each other and race to dad. Mom stopped us. The soldiers let him go and dad opened his arms widely and hugged all three of us. He squeezed us as hard as he could —we stayed like that for a long time — it felt miraculous. We cried — all four of us shed tears of happiness to be reunited again.

The moment our eyes met, was the best, the

160

happiest moment of my childhood. Before we came to see him, we learned that dad was very ill. We almost lost him. It was a miracle that he recuperated and is now sitting among us. We sobbed for a while, kissed and hugged literally a hundred times before we started any conversation. Dad changed a lot. He was always a slim man, but he lost a lot of weight and looked like skin and bones. Just like father, mother was never skinnier her entire life. Dad almost didn't recognize her. We were the happiest family in the entire world. Before we sat down, dad opened his bag, *"What is it dad? Do you have something for us? Did you buy a present? I think it is a chocolate!"* sis said. It wasn't chocolate, but it was chocolaty. As he unzipped his backpack, he took out two large Nutella jars. *"Yes! Yes! I knew it was something sweet! I knew it! Thank you!! Thank you Dad! You are the greatest!!!* Lamija jumped to kiss him. *"Thank you Daddy, you shouldn't have!!!I love you so much!"* I added. This was the second best treat, the second best gift I got in almost a year. The first one was dad.

The Concentration camps were to be "shut down" soon. The UNHCR was working on it, and it was a matter of time. We spent two hours with dad— then we had to go. It was heartbreaking—but we had no choice. As we were being forced out mom begged one of my father's ex-colleagues to let us stay a little longer. He stood motionless and speechless. Dad was taken by the same men—this time they were pushing and pulling him inside. Those two hours of happiness brought eight hours of tears. Just as we were getting ready to sleep, someone rang the doorbell. Aunt Aisha opened the door. It was Frank. He was taking handcuffs from dad's hands. His words were, *"I will come for you tomorrow at ten! Make sure you have yourself a goodnight!"* We stayed up the entire night.

We slept only few hours. I fall asleep like a baby, without any worries, fears or melancholy. The next morning I felt like the unhappiest little girl in the whole world. We had to leave.

With tears in our eyes, emptiness in our hearts, and pain in our chests we said goodbyes and left. On our way back, mom got really sick. She had to be taken in an ambulance to be operated in Zenica. One day ago, I was the happiest person, but the moment they took mom to the hospital because her cyst broke, I became the loneliest, the most depressed and most scared girl in the universe. Cousin Kamil came to get us. He took us to the house they were living in. Since they had little food too, Lamija was taken to stay with mom's family in Zenica. I stayed with Aunt Asya for a couple of days. These days were the most difficult days of my childhood. I used to wait for everyone to fall asleep and cry covering my mouth trying not to make, any noise...One night, I wrote:

Dear God,

Please have mercy on me and my family!!Please return my father, my sister and my mother to me. I promise I will be good. I promise not to do anything that might anger you and make you mad. I am so lonely. I am so sad. If you don't bring us back together, I don't know if I will be able to live alone. I don't have any more strength with me. I am starting to think that death might be better than this. Maybe Ajna's mother was right after all? Maybe we deserve this? We are bad, that is why these things are happening to us? I know that taking own life is unacceptable but sometimes I feel like it might be the best? Dear God bring back hope and faith to me. Give me a sign that everything will be ok. Show me that you love me by reuniting me with my family! Please let me see light through this darkness!"

A very lonely, and unhappy, nine-year-old girl

Two weeks later, a miracle happened. Mama got better. They were about to send her home, but this wasn't the only miracle. The news that dad was going to be freed came too. Soon my prayers were answered. Mama was still in the hospital on the March 31, 1994. This is my father's second birth day—the day dad was freed—the day the concentration camp doors in Zepce were closed. As he crossed the Begov Han's bridge, sister and I ran to him as we competed who was faster.

"Daddy!! Daddy you are here!!Daddy we are so happy to see you!! I knew this day would come! I dreamt of it all the time!! I knew you would return to us!!I waited patiently, and prayed every night!!Thank you God!!! Thank you for answering my prayers! Thank you for showing me the light!!"

I screamed as I sobbed out of happiness. I was relieved. I knew that now, that he was free, things would be easier. I knew my dad had "golden hands," and that he would try his best to provide for us. After mom was released from the hospital all four of us went to Vranduk.

CHAPTER 25:
Bosnia
April 1994-September 1998

Uncle Ahmed's grandmother had an old house next to his. She died. The house became empty, so we moved in. The house was so old that it was barely standing. Dad fixed it up as much as he could.

For the next five years we lived in it as refugees. The four of us ate, slept, and bathed in one room; a little bigger than a one car garage. This was the only "livable" room available in the entire house. The rest of the house was in terrible condition. Everything was falling down. The walls and the ceiling were full of holes and mold. There were mice all over. The house had no bathroom of any kind. It also had no showers, or a bathtub. We had no water in this house either. There was an outer water faucet with a huge stone-made tub.

We used to boil water on a slow combustion stove. The boiled and heated water was used to manually wash the dishes and dirty clothes. This, of course, was done outside, in hot and cold temperatures. I didn't mind washing outside during spring, summer and fall. However, I hated washing dishes and dirty clothes in the freezing, and below-freezing temperatures.

I wasn't forced or pressured to do it. I wanted to do it to help mom. She went through a lot already. When it was twenty-two of us in Aunt Berina's and Uncle Ahmed's house, she did the washing. Her hands looked like hands of an elderly person. They were always red and inflamed. There were no crèmes, no lotions, no medicine for that kind of pain, so she kept it to herself. Even though she never complained, I knew that her hands were hurting. I knew her feet and her back were aching due to all the standing, so I always tried to help.

We didn't bother Lamija with these things. We wanted to give her a chance at a normal childhood. There was an outer bathroom, or a squat toilet that had a hole in the middle of it. This wasn't like one of those modern, squat toilets. It was nothing compared to those. You couldn't sit on it. For someone who has never seen or used a squat toilet, it isn't an easy or a comfortable procedure. In order to take care of business, you had to squat over, place your feet on both sides of the toilet's hole. To avoid falling over, the feet had to be kept flat. This of course, was much better than taking care of business outside on the ground, in public, like we did back in the concentration camp, without toilet paper or a water bucket.

Here at the old house, I started obsessing about cleaning. I used to sweep the floors of the entire house several times a day. As soon as I would turn around, there, I would see the fallen paint, the straws from the wall and pieces of concrete. Then again... again... This only happened when I stayed inside, so I tried to spend all my time outside. I used to go to the fortress a couple of times daily. I couldn't wait to be invited to a friend's house for a lunch, a movie or a sleepover. I couldn't wait to be asked to tutor someone, or to study together with a classmate.

I used to wash the windows, at least once a week. I used to dust the house daily, but the smell of the old, for-too-long-not-taken-care-of house, couldn't go away. Cleaning and tidying it up made me feel relaxed. It made me feel as if I had control over something. Deep inside, I wanted life to be normal, like it was before the war. I wanted everything to be where it was supposed to. While I cleaned, I used to dream of living in a nice, medium-sized house, just like ours in Zepce — except for the fact that it wasn't ours anymore. Here I had my own room, bookshelves filled with books of all kind, a study desk, my own television and VCR set, and a nice comfy bed with a pink comforter and matching carpet. I imagined having a large bathroom and a large bathtub, with both hot and cold water. I imagined taking long baths, snorkeling in the water and playing with bubbles.

During winters, we used to bathe in our little room, in a plastic-mini-portable tub. The tub was slightly larger than one used for newborns, so small that you could only dream of getting inside it. We used to kneel down and with a plastic cup pour water over our head into the tub. Then after we shampooed and conditioned our hair, use the plastic cup to rinse our hair.

After we would finish washing our hair, we would wrap it in a towel, to dry it off a little. Then, we would take a cloth towel to wet our body; one by one, soap it, and wash the soap off with a cloth towel. This of course had to be done when everybody went out.

During summer time, we used to shower outside in an outer bathroom, just over the squat toilet. Here we didn't have to use a cloth towel. We were able to shower our entire bodies all at once. This was a better method of showering than the one in a mini-portable-tub. It was fine, except for the smell.

The outer faucet only had cold water, so we used to boil it and mix it up with cold water to make it more comfortable to wash ourselves. The house had no furniture. After dad was freed, he built a wooden sleeper. This became our sofa and a bed for four. In this room, we had our living room dining room, kitchen, bathroom and a bedroom. There was an ancient stove that started on wood. It had to be lit throughout the day.

During nighttime, we covered our bodies with extra blankets and comforters to stay warm. This stove was our heating and cooking unit. One of the neighbors gave us an old soft mattress. Dad, cut it up and put it on the wooden sleeper. We found some hard-hay-filled-pillows to top off our sofa-bed.

Most of the time, we had no electricity, so we used candles and oil-lamps at nighttime. No matter how much we cleaned, the place looked untidy. The paint, concrete and pieces of wood kept falling off. I used to help mom wash the dishes, and our clothes by hand.

One time, three of my classmates, the three smartest and the most popular girls from my class showed up unexpectedly to my door. As I opened the door, I was shocked. I stood silently not knowing what to say. I was hoping that they wouldn't want to come in, so I said to them, *"Hey! What a nice surprise to see you! How have you been? Did I forget something at school? Is there an assignment that I forgot to write down? Are you visiting someone on this side of town, so you just came by to say hello?"*

I kept talking nervously as my cheeks got red. I hoped that they would get the message and see that I wasn't ready to have people over.

"Hey Amna! We were on our way to the fortress. We took a walk. Since you live a minute from the castle, we decided to come over, and hang out at your place. If that is ok with you?" the tallest one of them answered.

"Of course it is okay!" I answered in a giggly tone. *"Come on in!"* I said.

They took off their shoes and walked into the big empty room, the one that was in the worst condition from the entire house. Thank God it didn't have lights, so they didn't see how old, and ugly it was. As we headed toward our room, they said nothing.

We walked in, and mom welcomed them. I made drinks for them. I mixed water with juice concentrate, and gave a glass to each. Mom made some homemade cookies, so I put them on the coffee table. I also popped some corn kernels and made popcorn for them.

They took a sip of the drink, and tried a small portion of the cookies. Finally, they tasted some corn too. They wanted to be polite. I think they even liked the snack and the desert that I gave them. I don't think they were disgusted by it. After all, this room was clean, and tidy.

Less than an hour later they left. They made no mention of the place where I lived. They gave no compliments, except for the cookies. We talked about an upcoming school event. I couldn't wait to have them leave. I was so ashamed, embarrassed, depressed. I hated this place. I felt as if I was judged for it.

I don't know how they felt, or what they said to each other afterward. Based on their gestures, and facial expressions, I noticed that they were shocked. I always came to school clean. I didn't have nice clothes, but they were always clean.

I was the fourth, smartest in the class, and the teacher liked me. My guess is, they couldn't believe that in spite of my living conditions, I was studious, and looked nice. They were shocked that someone could live in a place like this, be normal and smile. I noticed that they felt sorry for me. Just like me, they were embarrassed too.

They didn't experience concentration camps, bombings, shooting, and hiding. They didn't have to leave their homes. Their parents were with them all this time. They didn't know what starvation was. They didn't know what fear and pain meant.

This visit made them realize how blessed they were. After this day, they were nicer to me than before. A couple of times they invited me over. Never again, did they come to that house.

From that day, my self-diagnosed Obsessive Compulsive Disorder (O.C.D.) started, there — in that house. I cleaned because cleaning made me feel as if I was cleaning, washing off, erasing all those traumatic, unpleasant, scary and unhappy memories. For two decades, I had struggled with this obsession.

About a month later survivors from Srebrenica and Zepa arrived to Vranduk. It was end of July, 1995, when these unfortunate survivors arrived. They were the biggest victims in Bosnia and Herzegovina. Srebrenica is a place in Europe where the major human genocide since the World War II occurred. Those that survived were displaced all over Bosnia and Europe.

A large group of refugees arrived to Vranduk. They were stationed in a village hall used for meetings, parties, promotions, and things of that nature. We were the old refugees, and what we had gone through was incomparable to what these innocent people survived.

Mom became friends with a lot of women from Zepa and Srebrenica. The villagers felt for us. They pitied us, but they didn't go through things that we had gone through. The women from Srebrenica liked mom. They shared their stories with her.

One woman's name was Hafiza. She was old, in her eighties. Her five sons and her husband were killed in Srebrenica. Another women's name was Zlata, she was young and she just got married. She was seven months pregnant and her husband, her father and her father-in-law were murdered. There was a twenty-year old girl who was raped and pregnant. Her husband, her mother, her father, her brother, and her husband's family were killed too — and there was also that one — the one whose baby girl was shot while they tried to leave their burning home behind...

Back in school several new classmates arrived. Aliya, was the shy one, the quiet one. She was very religious and she spoke to nobody. She was an orphan — her both parents were killed in Zepa, and she took care of a younger sibling. She was very mature and calm, and she was extremely intelligent. We only spoke in school, but outside, she kept it to herself.

Maida, was two year older than me. She was the most beautiful girl I have ever seen. She had small hazel eyes, wavy honey-colored hair and big lips. We rode the bus together to school. The rumor was that Maida' saw her sister get killed and raped. Her parents were killed too.

Some of the refugees stayed in Vranduk shortly, and they relocated to be reunited with other relatives and friends. Others stayed there for years.

Even when Uncle Ahmed's grandmother was alive, the house looked like one of those abandoned places. There was something uneasy, and scary about this old place. People used to say that it was haunted. That it had ghosts. When she was alive, she spent most of her time alone. Not many people visited her. God have mercy on her soul, but she wasn't one of the friendliest people you met. She didn't like any of us, except for cousin Adna was the only one she used to invite in. Adna was the only one she gave some coins and treats to. From the adults, she liked none, except for mom.

170

While she was alive, my mom used to help her. Mom used to help her change her clothes, bathe her, cook for her and clean up, in exchange for cigarettes and some money. After she died, when I found out that we would live there, I was afraid. I used to think that she will come during my sleep and yell at me.

They called her Ada. She had gray hair, a big nose, and a huge mole on her face. When she smiled, which rarely happened, there was something scary about it. She was old and cranky, and it was hard to please her.

Many nights, during those five years, I used to be afraid to fall asleep. I used to imagine shadows. I used to imagine hearing noises, voices. Thank God, we all slept in one room. This is what kept me sane.

After we left Vranduk, whenever I prayed for my killed and dead relatives, I also prayed for Ada. I felt as if this was my duty. I felt that this is the only way I could repay her for living in her house. Perhaps, I also prayed, because I wanted to keep her happy. I didn't want to anger her...

We didn't starve, but we still struggled. This wasn't the most-desirable place to live in but we were happy. We were blessed to be together again, and nothing else mattered. Everything we needed for happiness was here. We had each other, and that was the most important thing. Everything else was easy.

After dad was released from the concentration camp, he found ways to feed us. Our starvation slowly disappeared. He used to make wooden farming tools for our neighbors in exchange for wheat and corn flour, potatoes, beans, green beans, peas, carrots, peppers, tomatoes, eggplants, cucumbers, spinach, apples, grapes, berries milk, eggs, cheese and sour cream. Sometimes, he even got us some chicken meat. In addition to making wooden trowels, hoes, pitchforks, rakes, axe handles, wooden doors, windows, chairs, cabinets, tables, storage boxes, he helped neighbors with any handy jobs.

Our first neighbors from Vranduk gave us a piece of their land located a couple of miles away. Here, we were given a chance to cultivate, plant, take care of, and use a piece of their farm land where we grew our own food. I used to love to pick potatoes, tomatoes, pickles, carrots, onion, and eat it fresh from the ground. There were times, when we went to forests, far away, to pick mushrooms and different berries from which we made delicious jam.

On July 2008, the Croats who occupied our home in Zepce moved out. The house was empty. The war was coming to an end. People were returning homes. A year ago, back in 2007, we decided to try to apply to come to the United States of America.

We knew that the home in Zepce wasn't burned or shelled down — but we also knew that we had no money to live to start fresh. Everything valuable that we had was taken.

How could we start anew? We needed money? Who could we ask? Those who had money weren't willing to lend it, so we decided to temporarily move back to Zepce and wait to see if we would be approved to try our luck in the land of dreams. As much as I was happy, I was also scared.

In school I studied German — why couldn't we go to Gemany? — My German was excellent — English? — my English was zero? Aunt Aisha told me not to worry. She said, *"Amna, you are smart, you will learn English in three to four months! Trust me! Your English will be perfect one day! Don't you worry about that!"*

A month before we left for America, we returned to our house located in Zepce. Our home, the same home we left five-years ago; the home dad wanted to burn, didn't look or feel the same. Even though everything was stolen, including my father's tools, furniture and the rest of our values, we fixed it up.

The war was coming to an end, and people started to return to their cities and villages. Everyone wanted to forget the war, to live in peace again, and to move on. Everyday people got sick of the hate, death and fighting; they were willing to reconcile differences and start over. Regular people from all sides lost. Only some profited from the war.

Lamija and I became close friends with a Croatian family; three sisters who, like us, had no faults or involvement in what happened. They used to come to our house to play, watch movies, listen to music and dance. We went to their house and hangout there too.

If we weren't approved to come to the United States of America, I would have attended integrated school with most Croatian classmates. I would have stayed friends with the sisters. Maybe, I would have healed from the war sooner? Maybe not?!

On September thirteenth, 1998 we left out mother land in hopes of starting a new life, in hopes of putting past behind and accomplishing the American Dream.

CHAPTER 26:
Chicago
April 2002

It was April of 2002. I was a junior at Taft High School. There were not many Bosnian students at this school. There was a group of Serbian students and a Croatian guy. The war was finished already a long time ago. All sides were trying to forget it, put it behind, move on, and make friendships among each other. I developed a good friendship with my Serbian and Croatian friends. We got along very well. We talked, we laughed and we joked. We stayed away from any conversation that would make any of us feel uncomfortable. We didn't mention war.

This was something that we all agreed on silently, without consulting with each other. This was a sensitive topic. It was best to not mention it. It was best to pretend like it never happened. After all, it wasn't any of our faults. Nobody asked us if we wanted it. Nobody cared how it would make us feel. Nobody thought what effect it would make on us. We were children. We had no part in it.

There were two brothers; Milan and Dragan. They were born and raised in Bosnia. They were Orthodox Bosnians. The younger brother's birthday was coming up. He was throwing a birthday party at his house, so he invited us. This was the first party I was to attend.

After the two incidents back in our other two apartments, I didn't care about parties and going out at night. I was attacked and beaten on my way back from school during daylight. My father also escaped a brutal beating, possible handicap or possible death from the hands of gang bangers.

I was busy with work and school, and I didn't

care that much about parties. I wanted to do well in school. I wanted to become "someone" and "something." I was too mature for my age. I didn't think like most of my peers. I considered myself a "geek" more than a "party–animal." I became an adult at the age of nine. I didn't care about crazy-wild parties. I didn't want to disobey my parents. I didn't want to sneak out my house. I didn't want to hang out with the "cool" kids. I didn't want to make my parents worry. They had enough of fears and worries. I didn't want to give them more. I had seen a lot.

If I had a normal childhood, things would have been different. What I really wanted was to make my parents proud. I wanted people to praise me, to talk about me as an example, as a role model. I was a good girl, and I wanted to stay being a good girl.

The war frightened dad so much. It made him become cautious. He was scared of losing us again. It made him mistrust people. It made him over-protective. He loved us so much. He almost lost us once. Now, even though the war was over, dad was afraid that someone might want to hurt us. We were hurt there. He lost us once.

We suffered, but he couldn't do anything to protect us. His hands were tied. Now that we were given a second chance, dad tried to keep us safe, protected, and united as a family. This is probably why he waited for me to ask "Can I?" I waited for him to say "Go."

Sister didn't want to wait. She asked. When we were given a "Yes," I was surprised. She didn't remember war as much as I did. It didn't have the same impact on her as it did on me. She acted older than her real age... She behaved, dressed and even looked older than me. All the teachers at school called her "big mouth;" all the teachers, except our Spanish

175

teacher. She and our Mexican friends called her "boca grande" (big mouth).

At the party, most of the kids our age were Serbian. Lamija and I were the only two Bosnians. No one cared. The party went well, nothing in particular happened. I met a boy, a Serbian boy, whose parents were killed back then. He was just another victim, another orphan of war. I felt sorry for him. I felt guilty, as If somehow it was my fault that they were gone. I wished I had a power to bring them back — I wished there was no war in the first place.

Couple days, after the party, dad asked me to go to a room to sit down and talk. I loved my dad. I respected him so much, but hated talks about boys, and going out. We sat down in our bedroom. Mom and sis stayed in the living room.

As I walked in, he said feeling uneasy, *Amna please sit down.* I had a feeling what this talk was going to be about, so I made an oh-great-face. I sat down and I waited for him to start. I had a feeling that this had something to do with us spending time with Serbian friends.

"Amna, you are our first born. You are young, intelligent, innocent and beautiful. I want you to know that there are lots of bad people in this world. These people don't have good intentions. They don't have good hearts, good manners. Some of them try to take advantage of young girls like you and your sister. You are so young and naïve. I know you know these things already, but I must repeat them for you. You are smart, and you know what appropriate and desirable behavior is for a young lady. I know that you are mature for your age. I know that you would never do anything to bring shame and embarrassment to our family, but it is my role, my duty as a parent to repeat and tell you this over and

176

over."

The more he talked, the more uncomfortable I became. I knew these things already. I hated when they treated me like a child. I hated when they repeated themselves. Without any interruptions I continued listening to him. I hoped for the talk to be short.

That is when he continued, "*Amna, you are about to turn eighteen. I think it is time for you to start dating, going out with friends. Maybe even having a boyfriend?*" I couldn't believe what I heard. "*I know how good you have been to us, and we are very proud of you! I know that I might have been a little more over-protective than I should have been, but one day when you have your own kids you'll understand. Your mother and I love you two and only want what's best for you. I am sorry for being too protective, but I only did it out of love. Forgive me for that! If you want, you and your sister could go out this weekend to a place where Bosnian girls and boys your age hang out.*"

By the time he finished his speech, my eyes were filled with tears, my armpits and palms were sweaty. Lamija and mom were outside secretly listening to our conversation.

My relationship with mom was unique. We admired our mom. We were able to talk to her about anything except boys, or sex. When we touched upon these topics, all we heard was "*No sex before marriage! Most men want to play with girls' feelings. They want to get them to bed. After they get them to bed, they leave them. When it comes to marriage, they want to marry someone who has never been seen or touched by anyone. Girls that lose themselves and give in are marked forever. Even if they get married, their husbands always bring up the*

177

virginity conversation, sooner or later. If a man truly loves you and wants you to be his, if he is truly the "one" he will wait and respect you for as long as he has to. Remember that my girls!" she explained. Mom didn't want to be in the middle, she didn't want to be responsible or blamed for any of our mistakes, and that is why she let my father do the talking.

The next weekend, our friend Anita, sis and I got ready to go out. We dressed up, did our make-up and hair, and were ready to leave. Before we walked out, I took one last look at myself in the mirror. As I looked in the mirror, I saw a tall, slender, young girl with a long-round face, light skin without acne or pimples, a high forehead, medium-thick curvy eyebrows raised above big greenish eyes and long, thick dark eyelashes. I wore black mascara, eyeliner, pinkish lipstick, and just a little bit of liquid foundation.

This was the first time I applied foundation on my face. I decided to let down my long curly brown hair with lots of blond highlights that I got just about a month before, after my mom, sister and I begged my father for permission. His words were the following, *"If you really want to get these highlights, go ahead. It is your choice. If you want to look different from what God made you, do it! If you ask me, natural is the most beautiful. If you disagree go ahead! I know that coloring and highlights only damage and destroy hair, but I may be wrong!"*

"Thank you daddy! Thank you! You are the best!" I answered happily, as I kissed his cheek. I never said this to him, but he was right. The highlights didn't come out the way I wanted them to.

I put on black pants. The dress pants were slightly tight, just enough to show my behind, and on top I wore a beige, V-neck long sleeve shirt, with a ruffle on each arm. I sprayed myself with an inexpensive perfume that smelled nice, and I wore my black high-heels.

Lamija wanted to wear a mini skirt to show off her good legs, but knowing the rules, decided to wear tight jeans, very high-heels that she borrowed from Anita, and a red short-sleeved shirt. She also applied lots of dark eye shadow, red blush, red lipstick on her bid dark lips and eyeliner both on her eye lids and on the inside of her eyes. She straightened her hair, and before we left, she looked at least four years older than me.

Just before we left, Anita, a medium-tanned, average-height girl, with huge brown eyes and thin curvy eyebrows, beautiful nose and big lips came in. She wore a black dress just above her knees and silver high-heel shoes. She wore eyeliner, light brown eye shadow, mascara, brown lipstick, and a little bit of blush.

She was a beautiful girl, and she didn't need a lot of make-up. She was an immigrant from Mexico, and unlike most Hispanics, she had pale-looking skin. Most people assumed that Anita was the Bosnian, and Lamija the Mexican, since she had brownish skin color just like my mom. From the moment I met her I liked her personality, her sense of humor and maturity, and I knew she was a good girl.

We exited our garden apartment. We climbed up the stairs, and said goodbye to my folks, as they were leaving too. They were invited to a dinner at their friends' house, so they left at the same time we did. As I opened the door of my used black Mazda Protégé, given to me as a present from my dad after he purchased a brand new silver Chrysler Voyager van, he repeated himself for the fifth time this evening saying *"Girls, you know that the curfew is twelve.*

That means not five minutes, not a minute after twelve. Remember! Back in my day, our curfews were ten. Hajd sad, pamet u glavu pazite sta radite" (Be responsible! Don't do anything stupid!) he said as I drove away. The reason why I was given a car was partly for my good behavior, but mainly because our high school was a couple of miles away, and walking during winters wasn't pleasant. Plus, in Chicago, if you had a full schedule and if you wanted to save time, you had to have a car; a car wasn't a luxury but a necessity.

CHAPTER 27:
Chicago
April 2002

Café "Una" was a place that I visited once with my parents, sister and cousins from Vermont. That night, including a few other times I went to Bosnian concert, I sat on my chair whole night. I only got up to go to the restroom. Sister would get up and dance to folk music, along with other girls and women of all ages. They would dance in circles holding hands and following a simple dance technique. I was shy. I couldn't dance. I was good at studying, writing poetry and getting good grades. I always had difficulty relaxing, and even though lots of people complemented my looks and said that I could be a "model" or a "miss," I never believed it.

There were a couple of reasons why I stayed away from dancing. As a child, my sister would innocently laugh at me when I attempted and failed at imitating her moves and moving my body the way she could. There was also another, bigger reason, a weakness I was born with, my sweaty hands. I avoided shaking hands with people.

Café "Una" was one of the Bosnian places in Chicago that had live music and a band. It was located in an older brick-building on the second floor in Korea Town, right on Lawrence Avenue, a block away from the Brown Line Station, just across the Salvation Army. As we neared the "Una," I had to pull up to the side of the street.

It was my luck that I drove over a nail and got a flat tire. *"Gosh...this is the last thing we needed! Great!!! I knew something bad would happen. I had a feeling that this was all a dream the moment dad said I could go out. What are we going to do now?"* I asked in a very upset tone.

"Let's call dad and ask him before we do anything" sis said. "Yeah that's right Amna, call Mr. Adem and ask." Anita added.

I took out my cell phone and dialed his number, "Dad, dad, we got a flat tire, just a block before "Una." What are we going to do?" Since it was only around eight, he said "Are you girls ok? Is anyone hurt?" my dad asked worryingly.

"Yes, we are ok, nothing happened. The car should be safe here," I answered. "If you want I can come and pick you up around ten, ten thirty?" he asked.

"Great!!!" ten would be perfect timing!" I thought to myself, "Whatever you say daddy. Ten might be little too early. All my friends at school arrive to clubs at ten, but if you say ten, it will be ten." I said with a face full of disappointment. "Ok, let's see. Go on in. Let's talk later. If anything changes I'll let you know. Ok. Pamet u glavu!" (Don't do anything stupid!) he added as he hung up.

We climbed up the stairs and walked in. The place was empty, except for staff and a couple of older guys drinking at the bar. The band was setting up the equipment. We walked towards the middle of the room and we chose a table close to the wall.

"Una" looked plain; there was nothing special about it. The table and chairs were old. The floors were all scratched up. It was painted in red color, and it had disco lights.

We sat down and ordered three cokes. Anita wanted a beer, but settled on a coke for now. I felt as If I also needed something to cheer me up, to relax me, and give me some confidence.

After an hour of being there, people started coming in, and the two singers; a husband and a wife

182

started singing some of the most popular and touching songs.

While sitting and chatting, Merisa, a girl that went to Sullivan High School with me, walked in with a group of people. Among these girls there was also this guy. She asked if they could sit at our table and we said yes. Soon people started getting up to dance, and all the girls from the table got up too.

I was left all alone with the guy, who appeared to have been in his early thirties. He had long, curly brown hair, big nose, big ears and a mouthful of yellowish, uneven teeth.

When he smiled, I noticed that one of his upper premolars was missing. His long hair was oily, and it looked as if he forgot to wash it for weeks. He had a small beard and a mustache, which made him look like he was in his fifties. His breath smelled. As he sat, he smoked one after another; puffing the cigarette, acting tough and trying to be cool.

I never judged people based on their looks, at least not until that night. I couldn't wait for the girls to return to the table to get up and leave this guy.

Ever since they got up to dance, he had been telling me, *"You seem to be a very intelligent and a beautiful girl. I'm visiting from Michigan, and I would love to get together tomorrow. We could go out for coffee? You are different than the other girls. I am looking for someone like you. How about the two of us hook up? This could be something!?"*

As he said these words, out of shock I coughed, and almost choked on my Coca-Cola drink.

"Are you ok?" he asked.

"Yes, I am ok, thanks!" I answered wanting to be polite; trying not to show anger, since I pitied him. It was not that he was so unattractive, at least not physically. His talk, his movement, his behavior and

183

his arrogance made him appear unattractive.

"Thank you for your compliments, but I am going to have to say "no." I am very young, and the only thing on my mind is my school and studies. I don't want to be in any relationship any time soon" I said politely, as I pulled my chair away from him, since all this time he had slowly been pushing his chair closer to mine. At one point, he even put one of his arms on my chair.

As I sat down, I silently prayed, *"Dear God, send them here fast! This guy freaks me out. I don't even remember his name, and he is telling me that he wants a serious relationship with a girl like me?! Please send them here?"*

Lamija and Anita were here sooner than I expected. They came to take a sip of their coke, and to tell me that they had met some girls who said they would give us a ride home. We called dad and asked him if that would be ok, and he said yes as long as we came before our curfew.

As they were about to go back to dancing, I decided to get up and follow them. I remember telling myself, *"Why do I think I can't dance? It is not as if anyone is doing some extraordinary moves? Nobody in this place is a professional dancer. As a matter of fact, there were some who made fools out of themselves, but they didn't care. Why do I care? I'll just get up and give it a try!"*

They looked at me with surprise, since they were both aware of my insecurities. They gave me a smile and a look that showed how happy they were for me. Walking through the crowd, they told me about this "cute guy" that they both were eying the whole night.

As I turned around, I saw the "freaky-guy." The next song was a song that people danced to any way they wanted to. That made me happy. I knew I wouldn't have to hold my sweaty hands with anyone. The "annoying-guy" joined us as we were dancing in a group of six. There was sis Anita, him, "the cute guy" his friend, and me. As I moved slowly, trying to relax to the music, I kept turning my back toward the weirdo. I wanted to let him know that there will be nothing between us.

The "cute-guy" kept looking at me, trying to get my attention, as if he wanted to get our eyes to meet. I noticed it, but I ignored it. I acted uninterestedly. As the song ended the "cute-guy" approached me asking, "Would you like to go sit down and drink something?" Lamija and Anita gave each other looks as if their eyes told each other "I knew he would choose her!"

There was something about this guy, something hard to explain. As I looked at him, I remembered seeing him somewhere before. *"Yes I know you."* I said to him wanting to start a conversation and end my uneasiness.

"Aren't you Belma's uncle?" I asked knowing the answer already.

"How do you know that I'm her uncle? How do you know Belma?" he asked surprisingly.

"Belma and I went to same school. We were in the same Spanish class. She was one of the "cool girls" She used to ask me to copy homework or to help her on tests. I always helped. We were pretty close to each other but our friendship was mainly at school. Outside school she had her things and I had mine." I explained as we sat at his table.

"What would you like to drink?" the waiter asked?

"I'll have a Heineken" he said.

"And I'll have the same" I added nervously,

185

fearing that someone might see me and tell my dad.

It is not that I wanted to disobey my father and drink beer, but I really needed something to relax me, and "make me cool."

As I looked around, all the girls around me, even the younger ones drank. Some of them drank not hiding, while others would take a sip every now and then, so that they wouldn't be seen.

"Once Belma had brought pictures, and showed me a picture of you. You wore a leather jacket and had the same hair style as Nick from the Backstreet Boys had, except for the hair color" I added. I remember Belma asked me if her uncle was cute.

The truth was he looked a lot cuter in real life than at that photo. He was very tall and slim. He wore an Express baby-blue-long-sleeve shirt with buttons, and Express blue jeans. He wasn't extremely muscular, but he wasn't skinny either.

I preferred skinnier guys; to me they looked younger than the big guys. I didn't have a perfect picture or expectation of "my-type of guy," but I always thought that he would have dark hair and light green eyes.

Jaan wasn't dark. He did not have light green eyes. He had brown hair and eyes that sometimes looked hazel, sometimes brown, and other times greenish depending on what he wore, the time of day, his mood and the weather. Yes, he was attractive.

There was definitely something about him, but at that time I remember thinking *"I don't think he is as cute as sis and Anita described him to be."* *"He is ok, but he is not all that"* I thought. After half a beer, I became more comfortable, more confident, and less shy. I also started talking more.

"So, what do you do? Are you in school?" I

asked.

"*I work at a hardware store as a salesperson in a plumbing department*" he answered wanting to change the topic.

"*What about your school?*" I asked again. "*Well, I am not studying at this time. I kind of had to drop out of high school*" he added.

"*What?*" I asked loudly. "*What do you mean you had to drop out?*" I insisted on finding out the rest of the story.

"*Well, when we came from Germany, they didn't accept all my credits, and they held me back. I was the oldest kid in my class and I was advised by one of my Bosnian teachers to stop going to school and get a GED. I stayed in school until I learned English. As soon as I did, I stopped going. I am planning to get my high school diploma, but I have been too busy. I will graduate soon,*" he explained feeling uncomfortable.

I decided to change the topic. We talked about our likes, our personalities and other fun topics.

Lamija and Anita were dancing in the crowd. Ever since I sat at Jann's table, I completely forgot about them. After my second beer I felt more than "buzzed." I was so happy, so relaxed, "so-cool." We got up to dance to a song.

As we were dancing, laughing and talking I felt as if the two of us were the only people in the room. For once I didn't think "what if..." and decided to follow my heart. For once, I stopped worrying and gave into my feelings...

As we were passionately kissing among the crowd, and as I opened my eyes, I saw my mother's cousin and his wife look at me... I looked down, feeling scared and ashamed, demanding to be taken home. I looked back at them, and I said nothing. I

187

wanted to disappear. I wanted to rewind the picture and erase them from the film.

The cousins turned around, as if they too felt uncomfortable. They were surprised. Jaan told hiscousin to go and get sis and Anita. We walked out toward the parking lot. He knew something was wrong, but he asked nothing.

"Jaan, those were my cousins. They saw us kissing. What is going to happen now? What if they tell my dad?" I said nervously. *Your father loves you and only wants to protect you. Those two, they won't say anything. They are in love, and they know how it feels. They went through this phase already. They know what it means to hide and do things that your parents don't approve of. Trust me. No need to panic. Even if they do say something, tell them I'm your boyfriend!"* he added calmly and confidently.

I looked at him with surprise. *"I came out tonight to have fun, not intending to find a boyfriend right away, I thought to myself. Hey, this might not be a bad idea after all. I'll say he is my boyfriend and I'll get to know him more. If I like him, we'll continue dating. If I don't we'll break up. People break up. That is normal. Next time I must be more careful of what I'm doing,"* I had a silent conversation with myself.

"Take my jacket, it is getting chilly. Let's get into the car. We'll wait for them inside" he explained. As we sat, Lamija, Anita, and Jaan's cousin walked in. They sat in the back. They looked happy. They had fun. They danced, they laughed and they enjoyed themselves. The "girls" that promised to give us a ride" broke their promise, so Jaan offered to drive us home. *"Yeah, you can drive us, but we must make sure dad doesn't find out"* I said. As we reached the alley of our building, we walked out only saying

goodbyes. We didn't exchange numbers, and we left it there.

We walked in, ten minutes before twelve. We were greeted by our mom. Dad was in bed already. She stayed up and waited for us to come. I tried to behave as normally as I could. I didn't want my mom to find out that I drank. I succeeded at it, even though my head was banging, spinning, and I felt as if I would throw up. Two beers were more than enough for me, but during the time we were in our room I managed to hide it.

"So, girls, how was it? Tell me, were there any boys?" mom eagerly asked.

"Some-one's got a boy-friend!" sis said singing as if I was the only one who kissed a boy.

"What do you mean?" mom added.

Due to the alcohol, I didn't really care that Lamija "opened her big mouth." Sooner or later they would find out.

"Who is he? What is his name? Where is he from? How does he look? Who are his parents? Tell me all about him" mom questioned.

"His name is Jaan and he has a good car! He is kind of cute. He dressed nicely, and he has a nice haircut." She answered. I just smiled. I let sister do the talking.

"Well, it is late, go to bed and we'll talk tomorrow," mom said ending the conversation. Dad was already in bed "sleeping." I couldn't fall asleep for a long time. I kept thinking about this guy. I kept smiling underneath my covers.

Next day called me to a room for another "talk."

"So, I hear from your mom that you met

189

someone? Is that true?" he asked. *"It is true,"* I answered nervously. *"You do know that I only want the best for you?! You are an adult. You are capable of making intelligent decisions. I don't want to be deciding for you anymore. I want you to make your own decisions carefully. I don't have anything against this guy or his family. Your mother told me that he is about five years older than you. I want you to keep that in mind. He is not a child, and most likely he is looking for a serious relationship. You are still young. You are still in school. This is only the beginning of dating for you. You have your whole life ahead of you. You shouldn't fall for the first guy. Don't rush. Take your time. In only a couple of months you'll start college and remember that school is the most important thing in the world, especially for a female. An educated woman has more options. She doesn't have to depend on a man. If she is unhappy with her marriage, she has something to fall onto. She doesn't have to suffer and keep up with it, as many women in my time did. You have a chance to make something out of yourself. When I was your age, I couldn't continue my education after high school. We had no money. I had to work. I only want you to use and take advantage of this. I want you to enjoy your life. I want you to be happy, to have no regrets. I am also aware of the fact that he doesn't even have a high school diploma. I am not saying that he is not right for you. All I am saying is to take your time. Don't rush. You do whatever you think is right. If you decide to continue seeing him, there will still be rules. The curfew will be the same. You may see each other up to two times a week, since you have work and school to focus on. Don't think that I am forbidding you of seeing this guy. I just want to open your eyes. That's all. One more thing, I don't want to meet all your boyfriends. I don't want you to bring them home. When the time is right, I will.* "he explained.

Just like the last time, I was in tears, this time, even bigger tears. As he finished I got up and ran to the bathroom. I walked in. I turned on water, and as I looked into mirror I cried as much as I could. My green eyes looked greener and lighter than usual. My face was red and swollen. I knew that he loved me. I knew that I was his little girl.

CHAPTER 28:
Chicago
2002-2004

The next Saturday we went out to the same place again. As we walked in, Jaan raised his hand calling us to go and sit at his table. We sat down and started talking. We talked the whole night. We exchanged numbers, and said goodbyes.

There was no intimacy. I decided to take things "slowly." Before we left, he told me that he was leaving to visit his two sisters in Minnesota, and that he would call me from there.

The next morning he called, and we spoke for two hours on the phone. My dad was at work, so we talked for a while. The following few days we talked on the phone again; each day an additional hour. The more I talked to him, the more I liked him.

I remember thinking, *"this is a guy that could win over my dad's heart. If my dad doesn't like him, he won't like any other guy."* Jaan was five years older, but we had lots of things in common. Our personalities clashed. We were different, but we were alike. After a week of talking to him I felt as if I had known him my entire life.

His calmness, his sincerity, his honesty, his simplicity, his patience, understanding, the way he spoke, acted and the words he said, the way he looked at me, held my hands, were all the attributes I looked for in a guy. He made me laugh. He made me feel secure about myself. He made me feel beautiful. He was almost "perfect." *"If only he would finish school... dad would like him,"* I used to say to myself.

He came to pick me up on our very first "date," the same day he got back from Minnesota. We went Zephyr, a nice restaurant located on Wilson Avenue.

It was nice and elegant. Fancy, but not overly fancy.

I was shy. I didn't want to eat in front of him, so we only ordered desert. We both asked for a banana split with chocolate, vanilla and strawberry ice cream. Mine came without whipped cream. I wasn't a big fan of it. His came with it.

After the restaurant, he took me for a ride in his brand-new silver GTI. We stopped at North Avenue Beach and paid for parking.

He took my hand, and he held it tightly. He didn't let it go. We walked for hours. On Foster Beach, he bought us corn on the cob, with mayonnaise. We sat down, and watched the lake. He asked for his corn to be hot and spicy. I asked for plain corn, with only mayonnaise and cheese.

There were people jugging, running, playing ball, tanning on the grass and fishing. Kids ran in all directions. Young lovers walked, kissed and looked at none but each other. There was so much happiness. We left some corn to feed the pigeons.

The more time we spent with each other the more I liked him. I wanted to be with him all the time. Jaan made me happy. He was the first "good thing" that happened to me since the war. He came into my life as a "savior" wanting to rescue me from the past, and wanting to show me the "good," and the "beautiful" in life.

I felt like never before; love was in the air. Every time I would see him, I would get butterflies in my belly. Every night I would dream of him and the nightmares started disappearing. I stopped thinking about the war. At school and at work he became the only thing on my mind. I started writing love poetry. I started writing his name over and over on all my notebooks. For the first time in my life I loved, and I was loved. My life was never better until now.

Weeks passed by. We spoke to each other on the phone every day, and we saw each other on the weekends. I tried to follow my dad's rules, and I did all until that day... It was Sunday. I worked as a cashier for a boutique at Golf Mill Mall. Sundays were usually the shorter days, and my parents knew that.

As I was leaving work and walking towards my car, there he was. Jaan wanted to see me and spend some time with me. I was eager to see him too. I decided to take a walk, and tell my folks that I had to stay at work late. Soon we left. He drove his car and I drove mine. We parked our cars in front of a bank located a block from my house. We waited ten minutes inside his car. We held hands, we laughed and we kissed. As I left, he kissed me and we said goodbyes.

I rang the doorbell and I was greeted by Lamija. Her face looked different than usual. Right away I knew something was wrong. I walked into our living room to say hello. Dad told me to sit.

While sipping a cup of coffee, he asked calmly, *"Where were you young lady?"*

"I was at work. I had to stay late. We got a new inventory, so I worked on the inventory sheet. I also had to open the boxes, and organize everything. Plus, we had a lot of customers, so I went back and forth. " I answered hoping to convince him.

"You were at work? Haaaaaaa? Who do you think you are lying to? Sram te bilo (Shame on you)!! Mene lazes? Mene? (Are you lying to me?) I brought you to this country to give you a better life. I brought you here to give you a good future, and this is what I get. You, out of all people disappointed me. I used to have high expectations of you. I used to trust you and you deserted me. You lost my trust!!!" he added yelling.

I stood still quietly, trying to control my cry as I cried silently. *"Why did you lie to me?"* he asked. *"Why did I lie? — I lied because I wanted to see him, that's why I lied"* I told myself.

"You don't know?!" he asked.

"I don't know why I lied," I answered. *"Well I know!!!! I know what I will do. The three of you are packing your bags and returning to Bosnia!!"* he said angrily.

"I'll stay here another year. I will work two jobs. I will save some money, and I'll come back too!!! That is what I'll do. There is no other!! How can I live and sleep peacefully if you lie? How can I trust you? What is the next thing you will lie to me about? How do you expect me to protect you if you lie?" he added.

"Dear God!!!I need you to help me. We can't go to Bosnia now. Not now. Please help me, please do something!!!" I begged inaudibly. This time, as if my prayers were heard, and as if God chose to side with love, I added *"Do you want to know why I lied to you? Do you? I will tell you the truth. The truth is I lied to you because I knew that you didn't approve of my relationship with him. I knew after our 'talk,' that if you do find out that I lied, you would stop me and prohibit me from seeing him."*

"You were right about that! I am not going to let you see this guy again!! Forget him! Forget about going out again! You are grounded!!" he added. I got up and I ran to my room. I climbed up my blue bunk bed, took a pillow and cried....

The next day he came out. He hugged me tightly, and kissed me on my cheek. This was his way of saying "I am sorry! I made a mistake! I was too protective!" I hugged and kissed him back. That is when he sincerely added, *"I don't know if you will ever understand why I was so protective. I hope that*

195

you can forgive me for that. I wish I acted differently. I wish I let you learn things on your own. I just hope that one day you will understand that I did it out of love. Dad loves you girls so much. You mean the world to me. I only did what I thought was best. I take back the punishment. Of course you can go out. If you like this guy, you have my blessing and approval to see him. You can see him as much as you want, as long as your work and school don't suffer. Instead of twelve, you can come home at twelve thirty!" daddy said with eyes full of tears.

I hugged him so hard, and I answered, *"I have nothing to forgive you! You did what you had to do. I understand you. I am happy to have parents who love me this much. I love you so much!"*

A year and a half later, Jaan graduated. He received his diploma and became a certified auto technician. We got engaged on Thanksgiving and Eid. Both holidays, happened on the same day. It was November 25th, 2003.

I didn't know anything about it. We talked about getting engaged. We agreed that his parents and his sisters would come and ask my dad for my hand. We were to follow the tradition. We wanted to do it the right way. His sisters were supposed to come, but something happened, and we decided to wait for engagement. I knew he wanted to marry me. I knew that the day he asks me to be his wife would come soon.

On November 25th, 2003, I got ready to go out on a date. He took me to Olive Garden, by Lincolnwood Mall. I fasted that Ramadan. The whole month, I kept thinking about the engagement. I worried what dad would say. I pictured Jaan down on his knees.

When he told me that his sisters weren't

coming for the Eid, I became a little upset. I didn't tell him. This was the first time, since we started dating, that I got mad at him. He picked me up at six p.m. I walked into his car. I kissed him on his cheek. I was cold.

As we arrived at the restaurant, we ordered Alfredo Fettuccini, Garlic Bread Sticks, and Italian salad. We had the best table, with the best view. He wanted to order a bottle of wine, but I said no. I wanted to wait a little. I fasted Ramadan, and I wanted to wait at least a week before I had any alcohol. We ate and we talked. I tried to avoid looking at his eyes, since I was mad. I felt as if the entire dinner, he wanted to say something. I felt as if he wanted to do something, but I ignored it. We finished dinner, and we walked outside, holding hands.

He opened the door for me and I went inside his car. The radio played romantic music. The singer guy was proposing to a girl. He was making promises. I pretended like I didn't pay attention to it. As I buckled my seat, I turned my head towards him. There it was! He opened the jewelry box and held a white gold diamond ring. The diamond was a nice size. It shined so much. This was the most beautiful thing I had ever seen.

"Would you marry me?" he asked nervously. I looked at him, and as a tear came out of my eyes, I went into his arm. I was shocked. I didn't expect it. I didn't picture it would happen like this. Not today. We hugged for five long minutes.

I sat silently. That is when he interrupted saying, *"Please say yes! Don't keep me waiting any longer! Be my wife and love me forever! Make me the happiest man in the universe! Give me the pleasure of waking up next to your beautiful smile and your gorgeous dimples for the rest of my life! Be the mother of my children! Be my companion, my love and my true friend! Amna marry me?"* He said as he looked deeply, passionately and nervously into my eyes.

"Yes, silly! Of course I will marry you!! You are my first and my last love! There is no one in this world I would want to spend the rest of my life with. You fulfill me! You make me laugh! You bring happiness and joy to my heart! Thanks to you I learned to love and live. Thanks to you I was able to move on. I was able to leave the war behind me. I learned to believe in love. I learned to believe in dreams, once again. I learned to believe in myself. I owe it all to you! Thank you for showing me happiness. Thank you for showing me that life can be good and beautiful!" I answered.

The day after we got engaged, my dad and Jaan met for the first time. Six months later, we became husband and wife. All I know is that, if I could go back in time, and choose any man to be my husband, I would choose the same. Jaan became not only love of my life, but my confident, my companion and my best friend.

CHAPTER 29:
Bosnia

Sarajevo looked enchanting from above. The sky was blue and clear as a calm ocean. The hills surrounding the city were olive, emerald, jade, pine, green, khaki and avocado green. The buildings and houses looked so small comparing to those in Chicago — everything was so close together. We saw roads going up and down the hills, mosques, churches and synagogues, restaurants, libraries, hospitals, schools, universities, offices, banks, supermarkets, shopping centers, cars, bikes, trains and people walking down the streets. Everything looked tiny from the sky.

The plane landed on the International Airport. I've waited for this day for years. Jaan, Hana, Sara, mom, dad, Lamija, her husband Mahir, her son Emrah, my cousin Kamil, his wife Saida and their daughter Edina, my Aunt Berina and Uncle Ahmed their youngest son Aydin, Aunt Berina's oldest son Adnan and his wife Amila, his sister Adna, Adna's husband Jasmin, her daughter Emina and I stepped out carrying our baggage.

The air felt pleasant. The wind touched our faces and made us feel welcomed. The kids ran off. They laughed and played with each other. They were amazed by "Bosnia" — it didn't look like the Bosnia and Herzegovina, described by their mommies and daddies during the period of darkness. People weren't sad. They didn't look poor. There wasn't any blood on the streets or ground. Everyone dressed stylishly, and everyone smiled. The buildings were remodeled; the homes were rebuilt. Everything looked normal and orderly.

We checked out our bags, and anxiously awaited our exiting the airport. Grandma Zineta who was in her eighties was waiting to see her great-grandkids for the first time. Yasin, Aunt Asya, Aunt Amina, Samia and her family, Aunt Najla, and Uncle Nail, his wife Irma, Aunt Sheila, Aunt Senada, Adan his wife Amela and his daughter Ilma, Harun, Amir and his wife Dina, Amel, Ajla her husband Haris and her son Ali, Aunt Aisha and her son Edin waited for us. Eleven years had passed since I had seen them. We ran to each other — we started kissing and hugging and introducing the newest members of our families. There was so much happiness — so many tears of pleasure and — so many tears of grief...

We took a bus to Zepce. First we went to the cemetery to pay our respects to those that were no longer with us — Grandfather Adil, Grandmother Fatima, Grandfather Asim, Uncle Onur, Aunt Leila, Uncle Besim, Uncle Muhamed, Uncle Hadis, Uncle Smail, and Uncle Enes, and Uncle Said.

We crouched and said our prayers in Arabic. There were so many tears — so much grief — words couldn't describe it. Zepce was filled with gray and black clouds. The sky was dark and gloomy. The air felt heavy and sticky on our skins. There were no signs of sun — it was around 2:00 p.m. — but it felt like night.

As we said *"Amin"* and we wiped off our tears, the sky opened — and the massive loads of water poured down upon us. The rain felt refreshing, rejuvenating. Then I looked up in the sky — through the darkness of the clouds — there it was, a yellowish light coming through. We stood motionless watching the sky till it stopped raining. The kids waited for us in the car.

Later, we went to a newly remodeled restaurant called "The Light." We entered the largest room. There was a buffet of gourmet food. Burek, Sirnica,

Zeljanica, Sarma, Punjene Paprike, Cevapi, Roasted Lamb, Bosanski Lonac, Salads, Soups, Baklava, Cakes, Fruit Salads and so much more. Twenty years ago, we dreamt of this much food.

We sat and we talked about the war, and the affect it had on us. We talked about those days when we had nothing to eat. We talked about those nights when we went to bed without supper. We talked about Aunt Leila, Uncle Muhamed, Onur, Nana Fatima, Enes, Besim, Hadis, Said, Smail...

The next day we woke up early. We drank coffee and we gathered in front of the place where twenty years ago we were imprisoned. White back and brown horses with carriages waited for us. We got in and we left.

We rode through Zeleca, Golubnje, Begov Han, Topcic Polje, and Nemila. As we approached the tunnels – for the first time I felt safe — not terrified — not shaking — not sweating.

Jaan, and Sara sat next to each other. Hana was sitting next to me. Our carriage with the whitest horse led the rest. The horse looked just like the one from my dreams —except for the wings — but it could fly. We flew through the tunnels feeling ecstasy, as if we were in the sky. The girls tickled each other and sang *"If you're happy and you know it clap your hands..."* We joined them and four of us sang and participated in a song.

Jaan couldn't keep his eyes off of me. He looked at me the same way he watched me that night in "Una" — the same way he looked at me the night he proposed. He looked at me the same way he did when we danced in White Eagle at our Wedding Reception— when they pronounced us a husband and a wife at Mosque in Northbrook— when we were on our honeymoon in Ft. Lauderdale—and the same way he looked at me as he held Hana as Sara the first time.

I looked back at him feeling shy, just like I did back then. I felt as If we just met. I felt as if he was seducing me all over. My cheeks were red. I was blushing and I had butterflies in my belly.

The tunnels were bright. They were painted nicely. They looked nothing like they did back then. As we stepped out of the second tunnel, at least hundreds of people familiar to me waited and clapped, sang and waved at us.

I was shocked. I didn't expect them there. All those neighbors from Vranduk — all those classmates — all those people I knew came out. I was speechless. Hana and Sara were amazed by the beauty of this country and the friendliness of people.

We rode through the tunnel, passed by the cemetery. We said our prayers and we stopped just behind the fortress.

Holding hands, the four of us, being followed by the rest of the family, we walked up the fortress slowly. Each step we made, I felt closer to that feeling I waited for decades. As we walked up the small hill we entered the enchanting fortress.

We walked up the walls cautiously. Jaan carried Sara, and I held Hana's hand. We stopped as we got to the point where you could see the other side of Vranduk — the school, the river, the hills, the house where I lived for five years as a refugee — the mosque — and good-hearted people.

I raised both of my arms to shoulder level. I closed my eyes and I focused on my breathing. I meditated. The air felt refreshing, and the wind made me giggle — that is when that same dream that I had over and over finally made sense...

"Mommy! Mommy! Look up in the sky! Can't you see the smiley face looking down at us!"

202

"I do my dearests!" — I smiled as I kissed and took into my arms Sara and Hana. Jaan joined us. We stood looking down the fortress feeling free. The rest of the family waved at us from bellow as they walked up the fortress.

The End

Made in the USA
San Bernardino, CA
26 December 2018